SO-BZM-500

Margaret Hill, Harriet Hill,
Richard Baggé, Pat Miersma

Healing the Wounds of Trauma

How the Church Can Help

Revised Edition 2009

Paulines Publications Africa

HEALING THE WOUNDS OF TRAUMA
© Wycliffe Africa, P.O. Box 44456, Nairobi 00100 Kenya
ISBN 9966-21-792-4
Year of publication 2004
1st reprint 2005
Revised edition 2009

PAULINES PUBLICATIONS AFRICA
Daughters of St Paul
P.O. Box 49026
00100 Nairobi GPO (Kenya)

Typesetting and Layout by Mukundi Miringu

Cover Design by Lawrence Mbugua

Printed by Progress Printers, 1445 Woodmere Ave., Traverse City, MI 49686

CONTENTS

DEDICATION

To the Church in Africa

"The LORD is near to those who are discouraged;
he saves those who have lost all hope."
(Ps 34:18)

ACKNOWLEDGEMENTS

This book was inspired by Rhiannon Lloyd and Kristine Bresser's book, *Healing the Wounds of Ethnic Conflict: the Role of the Church in Healing, Forgiveness and Reconciliation* (printed in 1998, unpublished). Ideas from that book are used with the author's permission, and that of Mercy Ministries International, CP 442, 1215 Geneva 15, Switzerland.

These materials were first used in the Ngbaka community in Northwest DRC. They were then revised and expanded at a workshop sponsored by the Institute for the Study of African Realities, May 2001. Participants at that workshop came from East African countries that had experienced trauma and war. Other participants had expertise in trauma healing: Karl Dortzbach *(Institute for the Study of African Realities)*, Joyce Fiodembo *(Counsellor, Nairobi)*, Emmie Gichinga *(Counsellor at GEM Counselling Services)*, Violette Nyrarukundo *(Counsellor, Kigali)*, Anastasse Sabamungu *(Coordinator, AEE Trauma Healing Programme, Kigali)*.

At a second workshop in March 2002, the materials were taught to pastors from six war torn areas in Africa, and translated into their mother tongues. These participants led local workshops using the materials, and reported back at a third workshop in April 2003. The materials were further refined and are now ready for wider use. We acknowledge the help of Cindy Langermann and Kathie Watters at these workshops, as well as artwork from Joyce Hyde, SIL International.

Scripture quotations are taken from the Good News Bible ©American Bible Society.

INTRODUCTION

In many parts of the world today, wars, ethnic conflict and civil disturbances, crime and natural disasters have left people traumatised. Often those traumatised are Christians, and the church has a clear responsibility to care for them. Beyond the church, Christians are to be light and salt in the world. This is particularly important in times of conflict and suffering.

The Scriptures are included throughout this book because it is the knowledge of God, his character and his relationship to people that are the foundation for healing. There are many places in the Bible that speak of his people suffering. For example, suffering is one of the main themes in certain epistles. The Psalmists are able to express how they feel in times of suffering. The whole book of Job treats the problem of innocent people suffering.

This book seeks to help church leaders who are called upon to help members in their congregations after major trauma has occurred. These traumas can include among other things, actions committed during war, criminal activity, and traumas as a result of natural disasters such as floods, landslides, and storms. These things may happen to whole communities, to families or to individuals. Though this book focuses on events happening to entire communities related to civil unrest, the same principles can be used in helping people in other difficulties. The book will also help individuals who are struggling with the issues surrounding suffering. The information in each lesson gives basic counselling principles within a biblical framework.

God's word speaks most deeply to people in the language of their hearts. The intention of the authors of this book is that it be translated into the language of the people where it is used, and that the Scriptures in the local language be used.

HOW TO USE THIS BOOK

This book is normally intended as a textbook for seminars. Leaders from all the churches in the area should be included in these seminars, if possible. The highest church leaders should be taught first, and then they can teach others who can in turn teach others (2 Tim 2:2). In this way, the teaching can permeate an area.

Lessons 1,2,3, and 9 are the core lessons, and should be taught at all seminars. Lesson 1 discusses the questions about God that come when there is great suffering. Lesson 2 helps us to recognize that wounds of the heart need to be cared for, in the same way that physical wounds need to be cared for. Lesson 3 describes the process of grief that allows us to be healed from trauma and loss. Lessons 4–7 cover special topics that may be important for your community: helping children who have experienced trauma, helping women who have been raped, ministering in the midst of AIDS, and caring for the caregiver. Choose the lessons that are most important for your community according to the time you have available.

"Taking Your Pain to the Cross" (Lesson 8) provides a special time for people to experience God's healing of their pain in a very meaningful way. It is often done in an evening session, towards the end of the seminar.

Lesson 9 is a core lesson. It should be done after "Taking Your Pain to the Cross." It deals with forgiveness and repentance. If your community is torn by ethnic tension, continue with Lesson 10, which is on living as a Christian in the midst of ethnic tension. All seminars should close with the Final Ceremony which provides participants with an opportunity to confess their sins and receive God's forgiveness.

LESSONS	RESPONSE
Core: Lessons 1, 2, 3	
Optional: 4, 5, 6, 7	
	8 Taking Your Pain to the Cross
Core: Lesson 9	
Optional: 10	
	Final Ceremony

Another important part of the seminars is to have participants share the trauma they have experienced. They should do this without justifying themselves, accusing others, or giving too many details that might frighten others. The group can then pray for those who have shared. This brings healing and bonds the group together in a special way. It is often done in evening sessions.

Seminars may last from three days to a whole week or more. The whole book cannot usually be taught in one seminar. Take time to cover the topics well. Subsequent seminars can be arranged to cover the rest of the book and to discuss experiences participants have had teaching the materials to others.

You might not have time to cover everything in a lesson. Study the lesson in advance, and pick the teaching and exercises that seem most relevant for your situation. Feel free to change the names or details in the stories to make them more appropriate for your situation. You may need to prepare skits or gather materials for certain lessons. Lesson 8 and the Final Ceremony require special preparation of materials before you begin. Instructions are found at the beginning of those lessons.

The lessons should be translated into the local language in advance. If possible participants should receive copies, especially if they will be teaching the materials to others. If you do not have a translation of the Old Testament in your language, you will either need to translate the passages cited, summarize them, or take them from another translation in a major language. Where a passage is written out in full in the lessons, do the same in your translation of the book.

Participants should bring the Scriptures they have in the local language with them to the seminar. Take time to look up the Scripture references that are in the lessons and read them out loud. It is the Word of God that gives life, and that will feed people's souls. If participants are not used to looking up passages, leaders may need to give instruction on how to do this. This will be time well spent. You may want to give out the references for a lesson on slips of paper to participants before the lesson begins, so that they can find them in advance and be ready to read them without delay during the lesson. If people do not have a copy of the Scriptures you are using, write the passages out on a blackboard or on a large piece of paper.

People learn best by participation, and for this reason these lessons are not supposed to be given as sermons. Section titles are often in the form of questions. Ask the group to answer the question. Then add any points from the book they have not mentioned. There are many exercises included. These should be done by all participants for the full value of the book to be realized. People remember 20 percent of what they hear, 50 percent of what they see, and 80 percent of what they experience. They will learn more if the leaders lecture less.

Each lesson starts with a story that depicts the problem the lesson addresses. These stories should be read aloud. Then there is the teaching of the lesson. Interspersed throughout the lesson are questions to be discussed in small groups. The purpose of these questions is to get the participants thinking about the subject and sharing their ideas. Their responses should be heard and understood, without elaborating on them. As you teach the materials, you can then reinforce what they have said, correct it, or add to it. Each lesson ends with a closing exercise.

Discussion can be done either as a large group, in small groups of three or more, or in groups of two. Vary the kinds of groups you use throughout a lesson. The small groups allow more participation by more people, especially those who are quiet in the large group. Each group can report a summary of their discussion back to the large group. Since it takes time for people to get into small groups, save these for longer exercises. Groups of two are faster to organize, as people can just talk with the person next to them. Generally, they do not report back to the main group. Use these for shorter questions. Remember, participation is key to good learning.

Lesson 1

IF GOD LOVES US, WHY DO WE SUFFER?

1. The Story of Pastor Yuh

In the country of Bingola, there is a pastor named Yuh. When Yuh was three years old, his father died and he went to live with his uncle. His uncle was cruel to him, beating him often and not letting him have enough to eat.

Yuh grew up and through help from another family member was able to go to school. He became a Christian and knew that Jesus had died for him. In time he had the opportunity to go to Bible school and became the pastor of a small village church. Two years later, war broke out in Bingola. Over the next three years, Yuh saw many terrible things: soldiers shooting innocent people, raping women, burning down villages. Finally, Yuh and his family were able to leave the country and settle down in a neighbouring country.

Yuh is still working as a pastor, but in his heart he is not happy. He keeps asking why God has let this suffering happen to his people. He is angry with God and feels that God has deserted him. Sometimes he thinks that maybe God is not strong enough to prevent these things from happening. Sometimes he thinks that maybe these terrible things have happened because of the sin of the Bingolan people, and this makes him preach more about the judgment of God. When Yuh preaches though, he often feels like a hypocrite because he preaches about God's goodness but really feels God is far away.

Discussion Questions

1. *What is Yuh feeling in his heart about God?*
2. *Why do you think Yuh feels this way about God?*
3. *Have you ever felt like Yuh?*

2. Is the God of the Bible Different from Our Traditional View of God?

Discussion Question

In our traditions, what do people believe God is like? Did he create the world? Did he then go away and leave it?

Cultures, like people, are not perfect.They shape our beliefs, but need to be evaluated in the light of Scripture so that they can be corrected.

Small Group Discussion

For each of the following verses, discuss these questions.

Psalm 91: 14, 15	*Psalms 103: 2-5,11-14*
Matthew 9:35-36	*1 John 4:9-10*
1 Peter 5:7	*Exodus 34:6 & 7*

1. *What do these verses teach us about God's character and his relationship to us?*
2. *How is this similar or different from our traditional view of God?*

3. When We Are Suffering What Do We Need to Remember about God's Character?

A. Read Romans 8:35-39 aloud:

"Who, then, can separate us from the love of Christ? Can trouble do it, or hardship or persecution or hunger or poverty or danger or death? As the scripture says,

"For your sake we are in danger of death at all times;
we are treated like sheep that are going to be slaughtered.

No, in all these things we have complete victory through him who loved us! For I am certain that nothing can separate us from his love: neither death nor life, neither angels nor other heavenly rulers or powers, neither the present nor the future, neither the world above nor the world below – there is nothing in all creation that will ever be able to separate us from the love of God which is ours through Christ Jesus our Lord."

✵ DISCUSSION QUESTION

What can we learn about God's character from this passage that will help us in times of suffering?

Sometimes when trouble comes we think it means that God doesn't love us anymore. This is not true. Nothing can separate us from his love. God promises to always be with us, even when we suffer (Ps 23:4-5; Heb 13:5b-6; Isa 43:1-2).

God still loves us.

B. Read 2 Peter 3:9-10 aloud:

"The Lord is not slow to do what he has promised, as some think. Instead, he is patient with you, because he does not want anyone to be destroyed, but wants all to turn away from their sins. But the Day of the Lord will come like a thief. On that Day the heavens will disappear with a shrill noise, the heavenly bodies will burn up and be destroyed, and the earth with everything in it will vanish."

✵ DISCUSSION QUESTION

What can we learn about God's character from this passage that will help us in times of suffering?

When we pray that God will stop a certain evil thing, and it continues, we must not think it is because God is weak. He is in control and hears our prayers. He is slow to act because he wants to give everyone time to repent, not because he is weak. When the time is right, he will powerfully judge sin (Ps 73:25-28; Rom 9:22-24).

God is all-powerful.

C. Read Psalm 34:18 aloud:

"The LORD is near to those who are discouraged;
he saves those who have lost all hope."

🏵 DISCUSSION QUESTION

*What can we learn about God's character from this passage that
will help us in times of suffering?*

Jesus understands our suffering because he suffered on the cross.
His suffering was far beyond anything we will ever experience (Mt
27:46; Heb 12:2-3). He suffers with those who are suffering (Mt
25:35-36). He is merciful and gracious even when we have doubts
(Isa 63:9; Isa 53:3-4; Heb 2:18).

God suffers with us and feels our pain.

D. Read Genesis 6:5-6 aloud:

"When the LORD saw how wicked everyone on earth was and how
evil their thoughts were all the time, he was sorry that he had ever
made them and put them on the earth."

🏵 DISCUSSION QUESTION

*What can we learn about God's character from this passage that
will help us in times of suffering?*

Not everything that happens is the perfect will of God. God hates
evil and injustice (Prov 6:16-19; Rom 1:18).

God hates evil and injustice.

4. Why Is There Suffering in the World?

🏵 Discussion Question

Why do people think there is suffering in the world?

The Scriptures tell us:

A. *Sin entered the world when Adam and Eve disobeyed God.*

Adam and Eve are the ancestors of all people. When they disobeyed God, evil and death entered the world (Gen 3:1-24). All people, Christians and non-Christians, experience the effects of Adam and Eve's disobedience (Rom 5:12).

B. *Satan has rebelled against God and tries to get us to rebel.*

Satan rebelled against God, and he wants to get as many people as he can to rebel against God with him (Lk 22:31; 1 Pet 5:8-9). He is a liar and murderer (Jn 8:44). Those who obey him lie, kill, and destroy.

C. *God gives us freedom to choose whether we will obey him or not.*

God created all people with the freedom to choose good or evil (Mt 7:13). He is grieved when we choose to do bad things, but he lets us make our own choices (Mt 23:37b, Rom 3:10-18).

Sometimes, even though we obey God, we suffer because of other people's evil choices (1 Pet 2:20-22; 3:14-17).

5. How Does God Use Suffering?

God's Word teaches us:

A. *God uses suffering to purify our faith.*

When gold is heated over a very hot fire, the bits of dirt in it rise to the top. These can be skimmed off, leaving the pure gold. Suffering is like fire: it is painful, but it results in purifying our faith in God (1 Pet 1:6-7; Ja 1:2-4). It makes us yearn for God's kingdom (Rom 8:18; 2 Cor 4:16-18; Rom 5:3-5; 1 Pet 3:14-17).

God's love is stronger than any suffering. In terrible situations when everything else is taken from us, we can experience the fact that God's grace is all we really need (2 Cor 12:9-10).

B. God turns evil into good.

Joseph's brothers sold him into slavery, but God used this experience to deliver the Israelites from famine (Gen 50:18-20).

God turned the greatest evil that was ever done into the greatest good for us all when Jesus was crucified on the cross (Acts 3:13-15; Phil 2:8-11). God works in ways we don't always understand, but we can always trust his character (Rom 8:28; 11:33-36). In the end, Satan will be completely defeated (Rev 20:10).

C. God comforts us in our suffering so we can comfort others.

God comforts us when we suffer. He holds us in his arms (Isa 40:11). He comforts us with his Word (Ps 119:50, 92). We can pass on this same comfort to others when they suffer (2 Cor 1:3-5).

SMALL GROUP DISCUSSION

Share how God has used suffering in your lives, perhaps in one of the ways mentioned above.

6. Why Is It Difficult To Believe in God's Goodness When We Suffer?

A. Childhood experiences can sometimes make it difficult to believe in God's goodness.

Children need to feel secure and protected from evil. If we have experienced difficult things as a child, we may find it difficult to trust others or God when we become adults. For example, if we grew up without a father or mother, or if our father was often angry with us, then it might be hard for us to believe that our heavenly Father loves us. The Bible teaches us that God is a loving Father (Jn 17:24; Rom 8:14-17).

A Loving Father

✽ Discussion in Twos

Think about your own father. As a child, did you experience your father's love? How does your experience with your earthly father affect your experience with your heavenly Father?

B. *Some sermons make it difficult to believe in God's goodness.*

i) Sermons that dwell on God's anger and judgment.

Sometimes churches teach a lot about how God judges us when we sin, but not much about how he loves us. It is true that God is all powerful, but we must also remember his great love for us (Jer 31:3; Lam 3:22-23; 1 Jn 4:9-10).

ii. Sermons that teach that we are saved by what we do.

Another dangerous teaching is that each person has to live a good life before they can please God or be used by him. We may think we are suffering because we haven't been good enough to please God. God's love is not based on our behaviour. He loved us before we turned to him (Rom 5:8; Tit 3:4-5; 1 Jn 4:19). He continues loving us by grace, not because of what we do (Rom 3:23-24; Eph 2:8-9).

iii. Sermons that promise prosperity for everyone who believes.

A teaching called "The Prosperity Gospel" says that if we obey God, we will always be rich and healthy. When someone suffers, this teaching will make them feel guilty, as people will say they have caused their own suffering. The Apostle Paul is a good example of someone who suffered a lot even though he was very obedient to God (2 Cor 1:8-10, Mt 5:19-21, Jas 2:5).

C. *It is difficult to remember God's goodness when we do not do the things that will help our faith grow strong.*

As we follow Jesus and study the Bible, we learn the truth about God and this sets us free from the lies of Satan (Jn 8:31-32; 2 Tim 3:14-17). Christians need to meet together for teaching, prayer, and fellowship (Acts 2:42; Phil 4:6-7; Heb 10:24-25). If these things are missing, we will find it much harder to believe in God's goodness when we suffer.

D. *When the church does not speak out against evil and injustice.*

God put the church in the world to challenge injustice and to help those in need (Lk 4:18-19; Mt 25:31-46). When the church does not do its work, evil increases, and people find it difficult to believe that God is really good like the Bible says.

✿ Small Group Exercise

We have talked about some things that may make it difficult for us to believe in God's goodness when we suffer. Which of these factors might keep you from believing in God's goodness when you go through suffering?

1. *Divide into small groups. Have each group make up a skit about one of the following topics:*

   a. *Adam and Eve sinning (Gen 3).*

   b. *God's frustration with people choosing to do evil before the flood (Gen 6).*

   c. *Joseph meeting his brothers and explaining how God used their evil for good (Gen 50).*

   d. *A child with an unloving father being taken into a new family with a loving father.*

   e. *Someone helping a person who has experienced suffering overcome their incorrect thoughts about God.*

2. *Experience God's love:*

   a. *Have everyone close their eyes and listen while someone slowly reads these verses.*

Lam 3:21-23	*1 John 3:1-2*
Psalm 103:13-14	*1 John 4:9-10*
Romans 8:14-16	*1 Peter 5:7*

   b. *Inspect your heart. Do you have any hidden doubts about God's love? If so, tell them to him.*

   c. *Think about God as your loving father. In your mind, imagine you are a child with your loving father. Sense the love in his eyes as he looks at you.*

   d. *Sing some songs about God's love for us. You may even make up new songs.*

Lesson 2

HOW CAN THE WOUNDS
OF OUR HEARTS BE HEALED?

1. The Story of John Mba

John Mba and his wife Mary lived in a small village in Bingola. They had two children living at home, and one older son who was in the nearby town working as a teacher. One night some rebel soldiers invaded the village and started setting fire to the houses. John, Mary, and their children ran out of their house as the roof caught fire. Two soldiers grabbed John, though Mary and the children managed to run away. As they ran, Mary looked behind and saw a soldier cutting off John's arm with a machete.

Not long after, they heard some trucks arriving, and the rebels quickly got into them and left the village. Mary ran back to John and was able to stop the bleeding from the stump of his arm. They went to the local hospital where the wound was treated and stitched. When their son in the town heard this news, he was horrified. After a little while John's wound healed. The rebels were chased out of the area, so life came back to normal for most people.

John began to learn to farm with only one arm. Although he did his best, he was angry with everyone. He started beating his wife and children, and quarrelling with all the neighbours. Mary was not angry with people but she felt very sad inside. She wasn't interested in eating very much, and often wanted to die. Sometimes when she was alone in the house, she became very frightened for no particular reason. Both she and John had trouble sleeping and often had nightmares.

The older son in the town, who had been a very good teacher, now started losing interest in his job. He drank a lot with his friends at night, and was often late arriving at the school in the morning. He had a lot of headaches and stomach aches, but the clinic couldn't find anything wrong with him.

All three of these people were Christians and went to church regularly. Every Sunday the pastor told them what God wanted them to do, how they should give money, and how they should work on the pastor's farm. One day, Mary began telling the pastor's wife how miserable and frightened she felt, but the pastor's wife told her that Christians should not have those kind of feelings. This made her feel ashamed of her feelings, so she never tried to talk to people again.

John's friends never talked about his missing arm. They just pretended nothing had happened. For John, his whole life had changed and he could not pretend that nothing had happened. John himself believed that men shouldn't talk about their problems, and he kept his feelings inside. The pastor knew that some people in his church had changed their behaviour for the worse since the troubles. He thought the solution was to preach more about God's laws

✿ DISCUSSION QUESTIONS

1. *What wounds are John, Mary, and their son carrying, in addition to John's physical wound?*

2. *In our area, what are some ways in which people's hearts have been wounded?*

3. *What does our culture teach us to do with our emotions when we are suffering inside?*

2. What Is a Wound of the Heart?

A. A heart wound is like a physical wound.

Read Ps 109:22. How would you say this in your language

DISCUSSION QUESTIONS

Think of a leg ulcer: How does it heal? What helps it heal?
How is a wound of the heart like a physical wound?

If possible write this chart on a blackboard or on a large piece of paper.

Physical Wound	Heart Wound
It is visible.	It is invisible, but shows up in the person's behaviour.
It is painful, and must be treated with care.	It is painful, and must be treated with care.
If ignored, it is likely to get worse.	If ignored, it is likely to get worse.
It must be cleaned to remove any foreign objects or dirt.	The pain has to come out, and any sin must be confessed.
If the wound heals on the surface with infection still inside, it will cause the person to become very sick.	If people pretend their emotional wounds are healed when really they are not, it will cause the person greater problems.
Only God can bring healing, but he often uses people and medicine to do so.	Only God can bring healing, but he often uses people and an understanding of how our emotions heal to do so.
If not treated, it attracts flies.	If not treated, it attracts sin.
It takes time to heal.	It takes time to heal.
A healed wound may leave a scar.	A healed heart wound also may leave a scar. People can be healed, but they will not be exactly the same as before the wound.

B. How do people with wounded hearts behave

✳ DISCUSSION QUESTION

What happens to the heart affects how we live. (Prv 4: 23)

Can you think of some people in your church who are showing unusual behaviour because they have bad wounds in their hearts? How do they act?

Some people with wounded hearts are always tense. Every loud noise makes them jump. They are frightened all the time, and expect another bad thing to happen at any moment. They may be so tense they can't fall asleep, or they may wake up very early. At times, they may shake or have a fast or irregular heart beat. At other times, they may have difficulty breathing, or feel dizzy or faint. Some people with wounded hearts are very angry, hateful, and can become violent. For example, women who have been raped may be angry at all men. Some people with wounded hearts are very sad and depressed and may cry a lot.

Some people with wounded hearts may avoid anything that brings back memories of traumatic events they have experienced. For instance, many people who have gone through a war in which airplanes were used in the fighting are now very frightened by the sound of an airplane. They may avoid airports. Some people who have been hurt by Christians may refuse to go to church. Some people with wounded hearts may not be able to remember part or all of what happened to them. (Ps 55:2-8)

Some people with wounded hearts feel numb. They don't care very much what happens to them. They have no energy. They are no longer disturbed by violence or seeing dead bodies.

Many people with wounded hearts find themselves thinking about the event all the time. At times, they may feel they are back in the event, re-living it again. This can happen while they are awake or in their dreams, as nightmares. Thinking about the event all the time will make it hard for them to concentrate on a particular task. For example, school children may find studying difficult.

Some people with wounded hearts may tell everyone about what has happened over and over again. On the other hand, some people may refuse to talk about it at all.

Some people with wounded hearts may try to kill the pain by taking drugs or alcohol. Others may eat too much or work too much as a way to avoid feeling the pain.

All these reactions are normal in people who have been through bad things like war. These reactions may happen immediately, or may be delayed and start happening a long time after the event.

C. What makes some wounds of the heart more serious?

Some situations are more difficult than others, for example:

1. Something very personal, for example, a family member dying or being betrayed by a close friend.
2. Something that goes on for a long time.
3. Something that happens many times over a period of time.
4. Something connected with death.
5. Something that people have done intentionally to cause pain rather than something that is accidental.

One person who has experienced a smaller trauma may react more severely to it than another person who has had a bigger trauma. A person is likely to react more severely to trauma if he is already:

- Someone who always wants someone else to tell them what to do.
- Someone who has mental illness or emotional problems.
- Someone who is naturally rather sad, or who is sensitive.
- Someone who had many bad things happen in the past, particularly if they happened when he or she was a child, like both parents dying.
- Someone who already had many problems before this happened.
- Someone who did not have the support of family or friends during and after the event.

3. What Does the Bible Teach Us about How To Handle Our Feelings?

Some Christians who have troubles like this say that we shouldn't think or talk about our feelings. They also say that we shouldn't go to others for help with our troubles. They say we should just forget the past and move on. They think that feeling pain in our hearts means we are doubting God's promises. This is not true!

A. Biblical characters share their feelings

 DISCUSSION QUESTION

What do these verses teach about handling our emotions?

Matthew 26:37-38 (Jesus)	*John 11:33-35 (Jesus)*
Matthew 26:75 (Peter)	*Jonah 4:1-3 (Jonah)*
1 Samuel 1:10, 13-16 (Hannah)	*Psalm 15:1 & 2 (David)*

Jesus had strong feelings and shared them with his disciples. Paul teaches us to share our problems with each other as a way of caring for each other (Gal 6:2; Phil 2:4). The Old Testament is full of examples of people pouring out their hearts to God: for example, Hannah, David, Solomon, Jeremiah. The Psalmist tells us that if we hold our pain in, it can make us sick. "When I kept silent, my bones wasted away through my groaning all day long" (Ps 32:3 NIV). God wants us to be honest and speak the truth from our hearts.

B. Laments

In Psalm 13:1 David says, "How long, O Lord? Will you forget me forever?" In verses 5 and 6 he says, "I have trusted in thy steadfast love; my heart shall rejoice in thy salvation. I will sing to the Lord, because he has dealt bountifully with me." How can he say both of these things at the same time? They seem contradictory.

One kind of Psalm is a lament Psalm. In a lament, people pour out their complaints to God in an effort to persuade him to act on their behalf, all the while stating their trust in him.[1] Laments can have seven parts:

1. Address to God (O God)
2. Review of God's faithfulness in the past
3. The complaint
4. A confession of sin or claim of innocence
5. A request for help
6. God's response (often not stated)
7. A vow to praise, statement of trust in God

Not all parts are present in each lament, and they are not always in the same order. Laments allow a person to fully express their grief, and even accuse God, but this is quickly followed by a statement of trust in God. This combination makes for very powerful prayers. The grief is not hidden, but the person does not stay in their grief – they call on God and express their faith in him. The laments encourage people to be honest with God, to speak the truth about their feelings and doubts. When they do, he can act.

In a lament, people do not attempt to solve the problem themselves, but they cry to God for help. They look to God, not the enemy, as the one ultimately in control of the situation. They ask God to take action to bring justice rather than taking action themselves or cursing the enemy (Ps 28:3-4).

 EXERCISES

1. Read Psalm 13 together in class. Identify the parts of this lament.

vs. 1-2: How much longer will you forget me, LORD? Forever? How much longer will you hide yourself from me? How long must I endure trouble? How long will sorrow fill my heart day and night? How long will my enemies triumph over me?	Address and complaint

[1]   Sixty-seven of the Psalms are considered laments – more than any other type of Psalm. Some were for use by individuals; others were used by the community together. The individual lament Psalms are: 3, 4, 5, 6, 7, 9-10, 11, 13, 16, 17, 22, 25, 26, 27, 28, 31, 35, 36, 38, 39, 40, 42-43, 51, 52, 54, 55, 56, 57, 59, 61, 62, 63, 64, 69, 70, 71, 77, 86, 88, 94, 102, 109, 120, 130, 140, 141, 142, 143. The community lament Psalms are: 12, 14, 44, 53, 58, 60, 74, 79, 80, 83, 85, 90, 106, 108, 123, 126, 137.

vs. 3-4: Look at me, O LORD my God, and answer me. Restore my strength; don't let me die. Don't let my enemies say, "We have defeated him." Don't let them gloat over my downfall.	Request
vs. 5a: I rely on your constant love;	Statement of trust in God
vs. 5b-6: I will be glad, because you will rescue me. I will sing to you, O LORD, because you have been good to me.	Vow to praise

2. *Laments are well known in many ethnic groups. They are a very good way to express deep emotions. Compose a lament in your mother tongue about your own painful experiences. It may be a written lament, a song, or a song and dance. Share your lament with the group.*

4. How Can We Help Someone Heal from the Wounds of Their Heart?

 EXERCISE

Do a skit that shows someone listening well to another person, and one that shows someone not listening well. Discuss what you observed.

People get pain out of their hearts by talking about it. Usually people need to talk to another person about their pain before they are ready to talk to God about it. If they are able to talk about their bad experiences, then after a while their reactions will become less and less. But if people are not able to talk about their pain, and if there is no one to help them, these reactions may continue for months and even years. They may get worse as time goes on rather than better. (Lk 6:43-45)

This talking can be done one on one or in a small group. The group should not be more than ten or twelve people, so that everyone has a chance to speak. The group could be a married couple, a family, or people who experienced a painful event together. If some people do not want to talk about their problems, they can be invited to listen. In time, they may be ready to share, too. It's important to find a safe and quiet place so that people can talk freely. Babies and small children should be cared for so parents can talk without being distracted by them. The group will probably need to meet more than once.

A. What is the goal of letting people talk about their pain?

By giving people the opportunity to talk about their pain, they can:
- Gain an honest understanding of what happened and how it has affected them (Jn 8:32).
- Accept what happened.
- Be able to trust God, rest in him, and let him heal them (Ps 62:8; 103:3).

B. What is a good listener like?

❊ *DISCUSSION QUESTION*

What kind of person would you feel free to share your deep pain with?

For people to feel free to share the deep wounds of their hearts, they need to know that the person:
- Cares about them. (Prv 20: 5)
- Will keep the information confidential (Prov 11:13).
- Will not criticize them or give them quick solutions (Prov 18:13).
- Will listen and understand their pain.
- Will not minimise their pain by comparing it with their own.

Pastors can identify wise and caring people and train them for this ministry. The hurt person himself should be allowed to choose who he or she feels at ease talking to.

C. How can we listen?

The listener should let the speaker speak at his/her own pace. It may take several meetings before the whole story has been discussed.

The following questions may help the listener to guide the person into telling their story:

1. What happened?
2. How did you feel?
3. What was the hardest part for you?
4. What gave you strength and helped you to get through it?
5. How did God help you?
6. How were you able to help others?

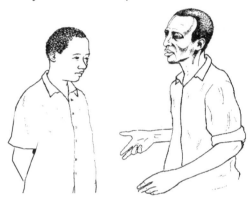

Show you are listening by responding in appropriate ways. This may be by looking at them, or by saying words of agreement like "Mmm." Don't look out the window or at your watch. Don't seem impatient for them to finish. It is important to be sensitive to cultural concerns as you listen. For example, eye contact when listening or speaking may or may not be appropriate.

From time to time, repeat what you think the person has said. This gives the person a chance to correct, restate or affirm your understanding.

If the person remembers dreams, encourage him to talk about them, and what he thinks they mean. This may be their inner self working through the event while they are asleep. It may also be God speaking to them in their pain. (Job 33:13-18) The meaning of dreams is symbolic (Gn 37:5-8). The things that happen in dreams should not be taken as if they occurred in real life. Commit any distressing dreams to the Lord in prayer (Dan 2:20-22).

When the person is ready, pray for him. Eventually, people need to bring their pain to the Lord themselves, but it will take time for them to be ready to do so.

D. Serious cases.

People who are very wounded may need more help than you are able to give them by listening to their pain. To evaluate how seriously a person has been wounded, look at:

- How many problems they have in the way they behave (see Section 2C).
- How frequent the problems are.
- How intense the problems are.
- How many months the problems last.
- If the problems keep them from taking care of themselves and their families.

People who are seriously wounded need professional help. If a psychologist or psychiatrist is not available, an ordinary doctor or nurse may at least give them medicine to calm them down and help them sleep.

CLOSING EXERCISE (1 HOUR)

Divide the participants into groups of two. Each person in turn tells about one bad thing that has happened – a small event rather than something very big. The other person listens. He must be careful to listen properly and to show he has understood, and is sharing in the speaker's pain. He should use the questions suggested in section 4C. After ten minutes, switch roles.
In a large group discuss:

- How did you feel during this exercise?
- Was anything difficult?
- Did you feel heard when you were listened to? Why or why not?
- What did the listener do well?

Lesson 3

WHAT HAPPENS WHEN SOMEONE IS GRIEVING?

1. The Story of Pastor Ndri

In the Boka district of Bingola, there had been fierce fighting. Many people had been killed, women and children as well as the men actually involved in the fighting. Ndri was the pastor of a large church in the main town of the area. As the situation in the area got worse, more and more of his church members were killed and those who remained were hiding in their houses.

Finally, one week almost all the people in the town fled from the fighting into the bush. Pastor Ndri went with a group of 100 people, and they decided together to walk to the next country where they thought they would be safe. On the way, Pastor Ndri's wife fell sick and because they had no way to get medicine, she died. Because of the danger, they buried her very quickly in the bush and then continued the journey. It took them three weeks to walk through the bush to safety. As they walked, more people became sick, particularly the small children and the old people. Six more people died before they arrived safely in the next country.

They were able to find a place to stay provided by a large church there, and they began to find ways of finding food and making some money. Soon more of the church members arrived to join them, and after a few weeks Pastor Ndri had over half of his church members there with him. They still came to Ndri for help and each day, and especially on Sundays, they met together to pray and read God's word.

Ndri soon became very concerned about the state of some of the Christians. Some of the adults who had lost family members were very sad and wouldn't try to find work, or even help to find food. They seemed to have lost interest in life in general. One man kept saying over and over again, "If only I had thought to take some medicine with us, my wife would be alive today!" One woman who had lost her husband was repeatedly telling everyone that she could hear her husband speaking to her. Another woman insisted that her son had not died even though everyone had seen his dead body. She kept expecting him to arrive with the next group of refugees.

Often Ndri himself had really bad nightmares and woke up crying out for his wife. He was also angry inside though he knew he shouldn't show this. He was angry with God, and even with his wife for dying and leaving him. He was also very angry with the rebels who had caused the war. Because he couldn't show this anger openly, it was burning him inside and giving him bad headaches and stomach ache.

✸ Discussion Questions
    1. What is Ndri experiencing?
    2. Have you ever felt like Ndri?

2. What Is Grieving?

Grieving is mourning the loss of something. This might be the loss of a family member or a friend. It might be the loss of a body part or the function of part of the body. It might be the loss of property or position. Whether small or enormous, all losses affect us and make us experience some degree of grieving. (Neh 1:3-4)

When people lose someone or something very important to them, they may lose their sense of who they are. This is particularly true when a spouse dies, or when someone loses a part of their body or sight. Through the grieving process, a person's old sense of who they are changes and adjusts to the new way of life. This takes time (Gn 50: 1-3).

Because Adam and Eve sinned, death came into the world, and grieving is part of the normal process of recovering from a loss. Only in heaven will there be no more crying (Rev 21:4). Because Christians have the hope of heaven, when they grieve they do not despair like non-Christians do (I Thes 4:13). They are sad, but they are not without hope or comfort.

3. How Can We Grieve in a Way that Brings Healing?

Grieving takes time and energy. It is like a journey that takes us through several villages, and leads to healing. (Is 61:1-3)

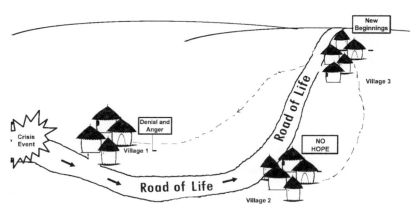

The Journey of Grief

A. The Village of Denial and Anger.

Village 1 is the Village of Denial and Anger. Just after people experience a loss, they are often numb and not completely aware of what is happening around them. They can't believe that the person has really died, or that the event actually happened. At other moments they may suddenly start to cry or erupt in anger. They may be angry with God, or with the person who has died for leaving them alone. They may have many questions such as, "If only I had done this or that, he wouldn't have died," or, "I wish I had…." Or "Why did it happen to me?" A person may also be tempted to find someone to blame for the death, and they may try to take revenge. This often results in conflict and broken relationships which increase the pain.

Sometimes people refuse to believe that the person is really dead. They think that the person is still there. Often people dream of seeing or hearing the dead person. This happens to people all around the world, and is not necessarily connected with evil spirits.

This stage may last for a month or longer after the loss. It can begin during the time of the funeral, and while people are still coming to the compound to comfort the bereaved family. The weeping and rituals of the wake and burial are helpful.

✿ Discussion in Twos

Think of a loss you have experienced. Did you have any of these feelings?

B. The Village of Feeling No Hope.

Village 2 is called the Village of No Hope. When people get to this village, they often feel sad and hopeless. They might find it hard to organize their lives. They still continue to long for the dead person to come back. They may feel very lonely and neglected and may want to kill themselves. It is possible that they may feel guilty – as though it was their fault the person died – even when there is no reason for this. The questions that started in Village 1 may continue.

Often people stay in this Village of No Hope for 6-15 months.

C. The Village of New Beginnings.

Village 3 is called the Village of New Beginnings. People who have accepted and grieved their loss can move on to Village 3. At this point they begin to think about making a new life for themselves. They are ready to go out with their friends and have fun

34

again. Those who have lost their spouse begin to think about another marriage. If they lost a child they may want to have a new baby. But people are changed by the loss; they will not be the same as they were before. If they have grieved well, they will be stronger people who are able to help others.

D. Not always a direct journey.

It is quite normal for people to revisit previous villages for a short period of time. Someone who has arrived at Village 2 may re-experience a few days of feeling very angry and then leave that behind again. Sometimes people may even start in Village 2 and then go to Village 1 later. Someone may have arrived in Village 3, but move back into the hopelessness of Village 2 in response to some event like the anniversary of a death. This may last for a week or so. All this is normal. Gradually a person moves more and more into the Village of New Beginnings.

What is not good is for someone to stay in Village 1 or 2 for a very long time. For example, a woman may still think she can see or hear her husband a year after he is dead. A mother of a dead child may keep his clothes ready for him, and won't give them away a year or more after the death. A man may still be unwilling to go to social events with his friends two years after his wife has died. These people have stayed in Village 1 or 2 too long, and may need special help to move on.

✻ DISCUSSION IN TWOS

In the loss you mentioned earlier, did you come through all the villages to the place of new beginnings? Do you feel you got stuck along the way? Did you loop back at all?

4. What Can Make Grieving More Difficult?

Grieving is hard work, but some things can make it even more difficult. These can be things about how the loss happened, or beliefs people have about grief.

A. The type of loss can make grieving more difficult.

Most losses need to be grieved, but these losses are especially difficult:

- When there are too many deaths or losses at the same time.
- When the death or loss is sudden and unexpected.
- When the death or loss is violent.
- When there is no corpse there to bury.
- When there is no way to confirm that the person has died.
- When the person that provided for the family has died, or the leader of the community.
- When the bereaved have unresolved problems with the dead person.
- When the death is a suicide or murder.
- When a child has died.

B. The false bridge can prevent people from grieving.

Some Christians think that since they have the Gospel and all the promises of God, it would be wrong to feel angry or sad about a loss. Some people call this the false bridge, because it appears to provide a straight path from the moment of the loss directly to the "New Beginnings," without passing through Villages 1 and 2. This is

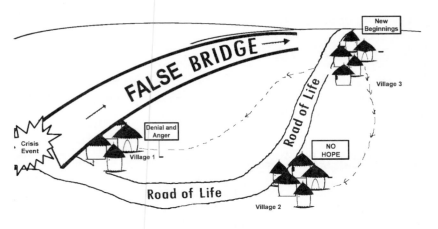

The False Bridge

36

not biblical, and it will not bring healing. God made us with the need to grieve our losses. Jesus expressed painful emotions on the cross when he said, "My God, my God, why have you abandoned me?" (Mt 27:46). He also wept when Lazarus died (Jn 11:35).

Facing the pain of loss takes courage. We are tempted to avoid it. Sometimes we get busy doing God's work as a way to avoid feeling the pain. This is dangerous, because if we do not grieve a loss when it happens, the grief will stay in us. It will not go away and it can cause problems for many years.

C. Beliefs about crying/weeping can keep us from grieving.

Some cultures require people to cry publicly when someone dies. Those who don't cry are suspected of not caring about the person who died, or of having caused the death. This can result in people crying dramatically, whether they feel sad or not. Other cultures do not allow people, especially men, to cry. This can result in people holding their grief inside rather than letting it out.

Tears are a way God has provided for sadness to leave our body. Weeping can be an important part of grieving, for men as well as women. Even Jesus wept when his close friend Lazarus died (Jn 11:33-38a). The Psalmist wept (Ps 6:6; 39:12; 42:3), as did the prophets (Isa 22:4; Jer 9:1). Ecclesiastes 3:4 says there is a time to weep. God notices our tears; they are precious to him (Isa 38:3-5).

People should not hold their tears inside, nor should they cry just for show. As much as possible, they should let their tears flow naturally. Sometimes the sadness comes at unexpected moments, even months after the loss.

DISCUSSION IN TWOS

Think again of the loss you experienced. Were there things that prevented you from grieving? What were they? Did your tears help let the pain out?

5. How Can We Help Those Who Are Grieving?

✺ SMALL GROUP DISCUSSION

1. When you have been mourning someone, what sort of helpful things have people done or said? What sort of unhelpful things have been done or said? Have some groups discuss the first question, and some the second. Then report back to the large group.

2. How does our culture traditionally help those who mourn? What customs are helpful? Which ones are not helpful? Are there any that would not be good for a Christian to do? Why?

A. The example of Job's unhelpful comforters.

Job was a wealthy man with a large family. In an instant, he lost everything: his children, his cattle, his wealth, his health. When his friends heard about Job's problems, they came to comfort him. They sat in silence with him for a week before speaking. Then Job broke the silence by expressing his pain. His friends were quick to point out his lack of faith (Job 4:3-6), and that his suffering was due to his sins and the sins of his children (Job 4:7-8). Although Job claimed he had not sinned, they were sure that if he were innocent God would not have let this happen (Job 8:6-8; 11:2-4; 22:21-30). They accused him over and over to try to get him to confess. Finally Job says, "You are all miserable comforters!" Rather than comforting Job, they increased his pai

✺ DISCUSSION QUESTION

What things did Job's comforters do or say that were helpful? What things did they do or say that were not helpful?

B. How can we help people in our culture who are grieving?

Some traditional ceremonies and practices help a person grieve. Others do not. Church leaders should encourage those ceremonies which are helpful and are in keeping with the Christian faith. In addition to these things, other ways to help a person grieve are listed here.

- Visit them. Pray for them (Eph 6:18).

- When they are ready, encourage them to talk about how they feel. Allow them to express their anger and sadness.(Is 61:1-3)

- Listen to their pain. Do more listening than talking. Healing will come as they let the pain out. They cannot absorb teaching and sermons at this time. (Job 21:2; Prv 18:13)

- Help them with practical things. If a grieving person has to worry about caring for themselves and their families, they will not have energy to mourn properly and recover. They might be too exhausted to do the work they did before, much less to do all the things the deceased person did. Relieve them of their regular responsibilities so that they can grieve. Especially at the time of the funeral and burial, there are many practical ways to help a grieving person. Widows and orphans are in particular need of help, and we are instructed to care for them: "What God the Father considers to be pure and genuine religion is this: to take care of orphans and widows in their suffering and to keep oneself from being corrupted by the world (Ja 1:27).

- Help them to understand that it is normal to grieve, and that it is a process that will take time. They will not always feel like they do today. It is important that they do not make major changes, like marrying someone, based on how they feel as they go through Village 1 and 2. When they are in Village 3, they will be able to make better decisions.

- If there is no corpse, arrange a church service to remember the person's life and to publicly acknowledge their death. A photo of the person or a cross can take the place of the corpse. If the family is dispersed, those who are displaced can hold similar ceremonies.

- It is not unusual for a person to have difficulty sleeping in the early weeks and months after a loss. If people are not able to sleep, encourage them to do hard work in the fields. If they live in the city, encourage them to take walks, or get involved in sports. Getting exhausted will help them sleep better at night.

- If the person denies that their loved one has died, gently help them realize it in small ways. For example, help the person to disperse their loved one's personal belongings.

- When the person is ready, you can read them a promise from God's word, and encourage them to memorize it, for example (Psalm 34:18, Isaiah 63:9, or John 14:1.)

- Eventually, they need to bring their pain to God. The more specific they can be about their loss, the better. For example, they may have lost a loved one, but also an income, companionship, respect, or security. They should bring these losses to the Lord one by one.

CLOSING EXERCISE

1. Divide into small groups. Using what you have learned, make up skits of a pastor visiting someone who has just lost their spouse. The skits should first show the wrong way to listen and then, in a second scene, the right way. Present the skits to the large group.

2. Art exercise: Have markers and paper or modeling clay available. Have everyone get quiet inside and ask God to show them the pain in their hearts. Now begin drawing or modeling clay without thinking about it, letting the pain come out through their fingers. Drawings may be symbolic rather than realistic. For example, churches may be represented by circles, or the dead by crosses. Each person will use symbols that mean something to him or her. For example, a cigarette may represent a brother who smokes. Allow 30-45 minutes for people to work individually. Then in small groups discuss what they have done and what it might mean.

Lesson 4

HOW CAN WE HELP CHILDREN
WHO HAVE EXPERIENCED BAD THINGS?

1. The Story of Kasi

A seven-year-old boy named Kasi lived in the Bokada region of Bingola. He was the child of a pastor and he had four brothers and sisters. When this story begins, he has just started school. He enjoys going off with his friends each morning. The teacher tells his father he is a bright boy and is already learning to read. In the afternoon, Kasi plays football and runs around with his friends and does small jobs for his mother until it is time to eat. He is a happy child who enjoys life.

One day Kasi notices that his father is spending a lot of time talking with the men of the village, and his mother is talking with other church women. He doesn't really bother to listen, but he begins to worry about what is going on. No one talks to him about it, either at home or in school. Suddenly one night, he is shaken awake by his older brother, and the whole family runs out of the house. He understands that some bad people are coming, but he doesn't know what they will do. As he and his family get ready to leave the village he hears some shots. He looks around and sees another family running after them, but their little boy drops to the ground dead. He doesn't remember what happens next but by the next day his whole family, along with four other families, have reached a place in the forest where some crops are growing.

Kasi's father takes charge, and everyone works hard to make grass shelters. No one talks to him about seeing his friend shot dead, and he tries to forget it. He has some friends in the group. They have fun together, and even build themselves a children's hut to play in. After a while one of the men starts teaching the children each morning. Every day Kasi's father leads prayers and singing with everyone, and they read the Bible. In the afternoons, the adults meet together to continue to learn to read and write in their own language. One of the women has even started a Sunday school. No one is really suffering from hunger, though they miss some of the things they used to have like tea and sugar. Every time anyone gets sick though, everyone prays very seriously to God to heal that person, because they have no medicines with which to treat him or her. Kasi starts to get scared of being sick. At night he has nightmares and cries out in fear.

After a month, a couple of men go back to the village to see what is happening. They find that it is safe to return, though the soldiers have burned down most of the houses, the church, and the school. They get back to the village and work hard to rebuild their houses. After a month or so, the school starts again, using a grass shelter for classes. But Kasi doesn't really want to go. When his father makes him, he gets into trouble with his teacher because he is not learning as well as he used to. He is scared to leave the house, and always wants to be with a family member. He jumps at every loud noise. At night, he wakes up the whole family with his screaming and crying. He sometimes wets the bed, though he never did that before the attack. He walks around looking sad and often cries. He used to like to play with his friends, but now he seldom wants to. When he does play with others, he wants to play war and pretend to shoot people. He often finishes up fighting with his friends. Every night he collects his things together in case they have to run away again, even though his brothers laugh at him for doing this.

Kasi's parents and school teachers don't understand why he is behaving like this. When he wets himself, or gets into fights with his friends, his mother beats him. This makes him cry more but doesn't change his behaviour. His parents don't know what to do with him.

1. How did Kasi behave before, during, and after the attack?

2. Why do you think his behaviour changed after the attack?

3. How do adults usually react to children like Kasi? Do you think these reactions are helpful?

2. How Do Children that Have Experienced Bad Things Behave?

When children experience bad things, they are affected in many ways. Many of these are different from the ways adults react.

A. Their emotions are affected.

• They may become fearful. Small children might cling to their parents. They may be afraid of strangers or of the dark. They may be afraid something bad will happen again. They may be afraid to go to school.

• They may become angry and aggressive. Small children may fight with their playmates more than before. Older children may rebel against their parents and teachers more than before.

• They may become sad. Even though a child is very sad, such as after someone dies, it is normal for him to stay sad for a while, and then play for a while.

• They may lose interest in life. The pain in their hearts preoccupies their minds. It saps their energy for life.

• Older children may feel guilty that they survived and others did not. Even adults can feel this way.

B. Their bodies are affected.

• Their speech may be affected. They may begin to stutter, or they may become mute.

- They may lose their appetite because they are anxious, or they may eat too much to try to kill the pain.

- They may complain of headaches, stomach aches, or other aches in their bodies. They may have hives or asthma.

C. Their behaviour is affected.

- They may go back to behaving like they did when they were younger. For example, children can start wetting the bed or sucking their thumbs again.

- They may have nightmares and bad dreams. Some small children may scream in their sleep without even being awake. This will stop as they grow older.

- They may play at war all the time.

- They may fight a lot and be irritable.

- They may cry a lot.

- They may be especially upset if they lose things that matter to them, like clothes or a toy or a book.

- They may do poorly at school because they can't concentrate.

- Older children may drink alcohol or take drugs to kill their pain, or become involved in wrong sexual relations.

- Older children may take risks, like riding fast on a motorcycle, or hunting alone for dangerous animals, or becoming a soldier. This makes them feel brave in the face of danger.

- Older children may hurt themselves, for example cutting their bodies or committing suicide.

✺ DISCUSSION QUESTION

Do you know any children who have experienced bad things? How do they behave?

3. How Do We Help Children Like Kasi?

A. Parents need to reunite the family, if possible, and re-establish routines.

It is important that families be brought together quickly after the bad event, if that is possible.

The more predictable each day's activities are, the better for the children. Each day Kasi should know what is likely to happen. He should be encouraged to go to school, help his mother, and play with his friends. Kasi's father was very wise when they were in the bush, to help the group have a routine such as: prayers in the morning, services on Sunday, "school" times, time for play, etc. Part of the activities should be having fun together. This may be playing games or, if making noise is dangerous, telling folk tales. It is important to try to finish activities that have been started. This gives the child the sense that they are able to accomplish something. It restores their sense of security. It helps them feel that the future is not out of control.

If there is tension between the father and mother, the children will sense it. Parents need to resolve any tensions there might be between them, for their own sakes and for the sakes of their children.

B. Parents need to listen to their children's pain.

Children know more about what is going on around them than adults realize. They tend to fill in missing information in whatever way makes sense to them. If they do not have a chance to talk about things, they may get very wrong, strange ideas in their heads. Even if parents are not used to talking with their children, it is very important that they do so when bad things are going on, as well as afterwards. This is not the time to say, "Go away and play." Families should talk together about the bad things that happened. Each child should have the chance to say what they felt when the soldiers came or the bad things happened. It is quite possible that some of the other children who are not showing that they have problems in fact do, and they should have the chance to share these. It is also good for parents to talk with each child individually.

Younger children are often better able to express things through play than by talking. When children play war, it helps them work out the pain they experienced. Parents should ask them about what they are playing and how they feel about it. Then they can go from talking about the play war to talking about the child's real experience that he is suffering from.

Another way to help children talk about their pain is through drawing. Parents can give them paper and pencils, or if these are not available, have them draw in the sand. If they don't know what to draw, ask them to draw a man, then their family, then where they used to live. Ask them to explain their drawing to you. Remember that the goal is to help them talk about their pain, not to teach them.

If children have bad dreams, explain that many times people dream about bad things that have happened to them. Encourage them to talk about their dreams. Ask them if they think their dream could be related to something that happened to them.

A Child's Drawing of His Experience of War

1. *Traditionally, do parents talk to their children in your area?*
2. *If they do not, what beliefs keep them from doing so?*
3. *How do these beliefs compare with Scripture?*
   Read Mk 10:13-16 and Dt 6:4-9.
4. *How can a way be provided for children to talk about their painful experiences?*

C. Parents need to tell children the truth about the situation.

A child needs to understand the truth of what has happened, in ways appropriate for their age. They should be told whether or not there is still danger and whether or not someone has died. Knowing the real danger is better than imagining all sorts of dangers that are not true. At the same time, parents should not exaggerate the danger or speak of all the bad things that could possibly happen.

Parents should make a plan for what they will do if something else bad happens, and discuss this openly with the family.

D. Parents need to have family devotions daily.

A good time to talk together as a family is at the end of the day. Each person, young and old, should talk about what he has seen or felt that day. Small children also need a chance to talk and to give their prayer requests. Then the family should all pray and sing together. Remember, as soon as children can talk to other people, they can talk to God. Bad things can bring a family closer together if they are handled in the right way.

Often small children do not understand death. They expect the person to come back. They ask questions like: "Why did God let this happen? Will he let it happen to me? Was it my fault? What will happen to the body after it's buried?" Some of their questions may be difficult to answer completely, but parents should answer as best they can and in ways that encourage the child to trust God.

Each family member needs to be helped to know that God is still there and cares for him or her. Each person could choose a verse to memorize, for example:

1. God is a watchman that never sleeps (Ps 121:4).
2. God can take all our fears (1 Pet 5:7).
3. God takes care of us like a person who takes good care of animals (Ps 23).
4. God is always there as our refuge (Ps 46:1).
5. God wants us to trust him (Prov 3:5).
6. God is gentle and patient (Mt 11:29).

E. Teenagers have particular needs.

Children between the ages of twelve and twenty are going through a difficult period of life even when there are no wars or other trauma. Some problems that may arise after a traumatic situation may be due simply to the age of the child.

Teenagers have a need for their own private space. This is particularly true for teenage girls. When families are displaced because of war, understanding a teenage girl's need for privacy can help, even if parents are not able to provide her with much privacy.

Teenagers have a need to discuss things with their peers, and this should be encouraged. Sometimes teenage girls are kept so busy in the home that they do not have a chance to talk with their friends. After a traumatic event, they need this chance to talk even more than normally.

Teenagers need to feel useful especially when their family is going through difficulties. If they can do things that help their family survive, this will give them a sense of worth.

F. Parents need to help teachers and school administrators understand what is happening.

Parents and other leaders should arrange a time to meet with the school director and teachers to discuss what has happened.

48

They need to understand how the trouble has affected the children and their performance at school. If the teachers understand the situation, they will be more patient with the students, and will be a part of the healing process.

G. *Serious cases.*

If after a year there is a child who is still showing serious problems, some mature, wise person needs to spend a lot of time with that child. God can heal the child, but it will take time. He or she may need professional help.

4. How Can We Help Child Soldiers?

In the world today, many children become soldiers. They may be kidnapped and forced into this, or they may choose to join the army for many reasons. For example, they may be poor and hungry, their family may have been killed and they have nowhere else to go, they may be angry at the enemy, or they may want to look brave in front of their friends. Any child (that is, a person less than 18 years old) who is exposed to fighting, killing, and seeing others killed will suffer trauma and will not develop properly as an adult without a lot of help.

Children who have been soldiers will find it very difficult to go back to normal life. They have often seen many evil acts and have learned to use violence as a way of solving life's problems. They may have been forced to do terrible things against their own communities or families. If possible, they need to return to their families, but this may be very difficult because of what they have done. People may be afraid of them or hate them.

They will need special help before they will be ready to return home and go back to school. There are organizations who run homes to help these children, and they may need to stay in such a home for some weeks. Like all people who have experienced trauma, they will need to tell their stories and be heard. Drawing pictures of what they did and saw, or acting it out in dramas will also help. Before they are able to return to normal life, they will need to know that people love and care for them (Ps 103:13-15). They will also need to repent of the evil they have done and know God's forgiveness. (1 Jn 1:8-9)

The church needs to help the community recognise the pain, loss, and trauma the child soldiers have experienced. Both the community and the child soldiers need to give their pain to God so he can heal them. They need to confess their sins, forgive each other, and be reconciled. The families of child soldiers may need help and encouragement from others while their child is integrating back into normal life. The child will seem a changed person to them, and it will take a while for relationships to be restored.

The church should also educate the community about the evils of having children serve as soldiers.

CLOSING SMALL GROUP EXERCISE

Read Deuteronomy 6:4-9 or Matthew 18:1-6 together.

- *Discuss how the passage challenges us in how we treat our children.*

- *Discuss what children in your area need special help and plan what can be done for them.*

- *Then pray together for these children.*

Lesson 5

HOW CAN WE HELP WOMEN
WHO HAVE BEEN RAPED?

1. The Story of Ama

Last year Bingola was invaded by foreign troops. Many of them took drugs and often got drunk. As they conquered the area, they often killed people and raped women to show they had power over the population. When they arrived in the village of Bagata, many of the villagers were able to flee before they arrived. Ama's family, though, was still in the village. Her husband George was away and it took her some time and a lot of effort to get her elderly, sick mother-in-law out of bed so that they could flee.

As they came out of the hut, the soldiers arrived. They ignored the old woman, but grabbed Ama and three soldiers raped her one after another. Ama tried to fight back so much that she broke her arm in the struggle, but they were much too strong for her. After a while, someone called the soldiers to help carry the loot away and Ama was able to run into the forest. She quickly found her mother-in-law, and together they tried to find the rest of the village. Ama was in shock, both from the rape and from the pain of her broken arm. After walking in the forest for hours, they eventually found the others. They helped care for Ama's arm, but she didn't dare tell them about the rape.

After two weeks they were able to return and rebuild their village. By this time George had returned home and his mother told him what had happened. He knew in his head that the rape was not Ama's fault, but because of what had happened he didn't want to sleep with her anymore. Ama felt so sad and awful that she thought about killing herself. After a while, she discovered she was pregnant. Finally she couldn't stand her pain any longer and so she went to talk to the pastor's wife, Mary. Mary was very understanding and listened well as Ama told her about what happened. As she talked she started crying and couldn't stop for a long time. Afterwards she felt as though part of the pressure and sadness had been released.

Mary asked Ama for permission to tell her husband about this, so that he could help George. Ama agreed. The pastor took time to be with George, and to let him say how he felt about the whole thing. As George was able to express his pain, and as Ama was beginning to find some healing, they were able to come together again and comfort each other.

Nine months after the rape, a little baby boy was born to Ama. George and Ama decided to call him Nathan, which means "Gift of God." By this time, many people knew what had happened, and some of them saw the child as a bad dirty thing. When the time came to dedicate the baby, the pastor arranged a very special service. He talked openly about the origins of this baby, and then said how the baby was a gift from God for the whole church. He asked them to stand up if they would help bring up this child to know and love the Lord. Many years later, Nathan became a well known pastor and teacher in the region, and his parents were very proud of him.

Discussion Questions

1. *Why did Ama not tell anyone what happened to her?*
2. *How did she find healing?*

2. What Is Rape?

Rape is when a person forces themselves sexually on another person without their consent. Most often, it is a man forcing himself on a woman or girl, but it can also happen to a boy or man. Even during times of peace, rape is a problem, but in times of war, it is far more frequent. Rape can be an act of lust or incest, or it can be an act of violence. Rape may be committed by a family member, a trusted friend, or a total stranger.

3. What Are the Effects of Rape?

✳ DISCUSSION QUESTION

1. Do you know of anyone who has been raped? How do you think the rape affected her? Her family? Her community?

2. Do you know anyone who has raped a woman? How has it affected him?

Rape is one of the most painful experiences a woman can go through. It leaves deep wounds in her heart which last for a long time. Because women feel ashamed by rape, the wounds it causes are often kept very secret. No one else ever knows what happened. Just because a woman does not talk about being raped does not mean it hasn't happened to her. (2 Sam 13:1-22)

A. How does rape affect a person?

- She will feel a deep sense of shame. She may feel covered with a dirtiness she cannot remove.

- She may feel ruined, that she no longer has any value. If she is not married, she may feel that no one will ever want to marry her. She may be very sad to the point of wanting to kill herself.

- She may be angry at all men. She may be angry at God for letting it happen. This anger may be let out on anyone who is with her.

- She may feel guilty and think God is punishing her. She may ask, "What did I do to cause this to happen to me?" Others may reinforce this feeling by accusing her of being responsible for the rape.

- She may be afraid to tell anyone. If they knew, they might accuse her of lying or blame her for what happened. Her husband or suitors might reject her, and the community may look down on her.

- She may no longer be able to enjoy sexual relations, and even become frigid (stiff with fear about sex). Or she may begin having sex with lots of men, because she feels that she is ruined and worthless.

- She may have injured sexual organs or other internal organs. As a woman struggles against the rapist, she may break bones or get other injuries. She could get AIDS, or other sexually transmitted diseases, or become pregnant. She might want to abort the baby. These things could lead to sterility.

- She may be unable to trust God to protect her in the future.

- She may think demons have possessed her.

B. How does rape affect the woman's marriage and family?

If the rape was done by a soldier or stranger, the family and community may be compassionate towards the woman. If they witnessed the rape, they may feel as violated as the girl herself.

If the woman does not tell her family, they will not be able to understand why she is sad and angry. Her husband may not understand why having sex is so difficult for her now.

If she tells her family about it, and the rape was done by someone they know, they might not want to admit that the father, uncle, brother, or pastor has done this bad thing. They may be afraid to accuse the rapist, especially if he is a respected member of the family or community. To keep the peace, they may deny that it happened and tell the girl she's lying. Or, if they believe that it happened, they might blame the girl for flirting with the rapist, and they may punish her. Or they may plan how to take revenge. In any case, rape will cause serious problems in the woman's marriage and family.

The woman's husband is especially affected by the rape. He may feel his wife is now polluted, and he may no longer want to be with her. When this happens, it adds to her feelings of shame and isolation.

C. How does rape affect the rapist?

Soldiers who rape often seem proud of what they have done, but the violence they do to others also kills something inside them.

If the man is a Christian, he may feel very guilty and ashamed. He will be even more afraid than the woman to tell others about what he did. He will be a man full of internal struggles. His shame may be so great that it leads him to kill himself.

4. How Can We Help Someone Who Has Been Raped?

A. She needs medical care.

The rape victim needs immediate medical care, if possible. There are medicines which can be given immediately after a rape which make it less likely that the woman will contract HIV, sexually transmitted diseases, tetanus, hepatitis B, or other illnesses. A doctor should check her for other infections and injuries, for example, broken bones or internal bleeding.

It is better if the person gets medical help within one or two days after the rape. Even if there is a delay, getting help within two weeks is still worthwhile. Somebody should go with the person to the doctor and stay with her there. This comforts and supports the person, and may help them give the necessary information to the doctor. This can be a member of the family, a friend or an older, caring woman.

✽ Discussion in Small Groups

What resources are available in your area to provide medical help to rape victims? If you don't know make a plan to find out.

B. She needs to have a person to talk to who she can trust.

Since rape makes a woman feel so deeply ashamed, she will only share her pain with someone she trusts to keep the matter private. Since rape victims already feel bad about themselves, they will not want to share their pain with people who reprimand or blame them more for what happened. Often the woman knows whom she can trust, and she should be allowed to choose whom she talks to. It could be a pastor, a pastor's wife, a wise woman in the church, or another woman who has been raped. Pastors can identify people in the church who are able to do this, and give them training to improve their skills.

When a woman talks to someone about her rape experience, it is very personal and a bond can form between them. Because of this, it is better if a woman talks with the raped woman. If a man is talking with her, it would be better that another woman be present. This could be either the man's wife or a mature woman in the church. If another woman cannot be present, his wife and someone else in the church should know that he is talking with the raped woman, and when and where this is taking place.

Some women will not feel free to share their pain with anyone. For this reason, pastors should include prayers and teaching for rape victims in their services. This might bring a ray of hope to someone who has deep, secret pain. It may also help them realize that they can talk about this subject with others.

The counsellor must enable the victim to talk openly about what has happened and what she is feeling. She should be allowed to say how angry and ashamed she feels. It is very common for rape victims to be angry at God. This is okay. God is able to accept her anger and still love her. It is better for her to be truthful about feelings than to hide them. Writing a lament would be a good way to get the feelings out (See Lesson 2, Section 3).

The first step in healing is when the woman realizes the impact of the rape on her life. This comes about by her talking about it and someone listening to her attentively and understanding how she is feeling. She will need a lot of time to talk about this over the following days and months.

1. If you had a big problem, who would you talk to?
2. What sort of people in your church could be trained to help raped women?

C. She needs to know that she is loved.

At first, the woman may be so angry at God that she is not willing to pray or listen to God's word. The only love she might be able to accept is that of those around her. By seeing that others still value and love her, she will gradually realize that she is not ruined. Her husband and family members can play a key role in this. Eventually, she may be willing to receive comfort from God's word and have others pray for her. Some Scriptures that might be helpful are Psalm 9:9-10; 10:17-18.

D. She needs to bring her pain to God.

When she is ready, she needs to bring her pain to God herself in prayer and ask him to heal her. The more specific she can be about what she lost in the rape – for example, her innocence, her purity, her joy – the better. She should ask God to restore these things to her (Ps 71:20-21).

E. She needs to forgive the person who raped her.

When the pain in her heart has been healed by God, then she can begin to forgive the rapist. He did a terrible thing, but God asks us to forgive those who do evil to us (Mt 6:14-15). The process of forgiveness may take a long time. If a child resulted from the rape, forgiving the rapist in her heart will help her more fully accept the child.

5. What about Children Born Out of Rape?

A. What are their special needs?

Sometimes, children born out of rape are rejected by their mothers and families. They may be treated poorly, or even neglected so much that they die. They may be ridiculed for not having a father. Their siblings may hate them and not consider them to be full members of the family.

B. How can we help these children?

God has a special love for the fatherless (Dt 10:18). In Psalm 68:5-6, it says: "God, who lives in his sacred Temple, cares for orphans and protects widows. He gives the lonely a home to live in and leads prisoners out into happy freedom, but rebels will have to live in a desolate land." As Christians, we should ask God to give us his special love for these children. They are not responsible for the bad things that have been done to them. They need our love even more than other children. They need special teaching from God's word to assure them that their life is not an accident. Some Scriptures that might be helpful are Psalm 139:14-18, Isaiah 49:15, and 1 Corinthians 1:27-29.

When they begin asking who their father is, it is good to tell them the truth. They most likely know more than people think they know. If the father is known, let them know who it is. If he is already dead at that time, it may be helpful to tell them who the relatives are.

The pastor will need to help the whole family to accept a child like this. The husband may find this difficult, and even older brothers and sisters may struggle with it. When the time comes for the baby to be dedicated or baptized in church, this is a good time to ask for a special blessing on the baby and the family.

✽ DISCUSSION QUESTION

Are there any children in your church who are teased or despised because of the events surrounding their birth? If so, how are you helping them?

6. How Can We Help the Rapist?

Rapists need to know that Jesus will forgive their sin (Isa 1:18). They may have raped more than once. They may continue to have a burning desire to have sex with women and think they can't overcome it. They need to have someone to whom they can confess their sin. This person needs to pray with them and keep them accountable for their actions day by day so that they will never do it again.

The rapist needs to take full responsibility for what he has done. He needs to ask his victim(s) to forgive him. Although he can never restore a woman's purity, he should do whatever he can to help her as a visible sign of his repentance. There may be legal consequences he will have to face.

If the church knows that a member raped someone, the pastor should talk to him about it. If he confesses and repents, the church should extend the same forgiveness God has given to the rapist. If he does not repent, he should be excluded from the church, both to protect other women from him and to bring him to repentance.

CLOSING SMALL GROUP EXERCISE

Imagine that Ama is a member of your church. She has told the pastor what has happened. How do you think your church would help Ama? Be realistic!

Lesson 6

HOW CAN A CHURCH MINISTER IN THE MIDST OF HIV/AIDS?

It would be helpful to have an informed medical person present during this session.

1. Two HIV/AIDS Stories

Didier and Mary's Story

Didier and Mary were happily married with four children. They were both committed Christians and knew it is wrong to sleep with anyone but your wife or husband. They'd heard about AIDS, but didn't really understand how you catch it. Didier was a farmer, and one day his village asked him to go to a course on better farming methods in the capital city. Didier was very happy to be chosen and went off for four months to do the course.

By the second month, Didier missed his wife very much and began to spend a lot of time day dreaming about women. At the course he had made friends with some other men who weren't Christians and they kept inviting him to go out with them in the evenings. So far he had refused, but he began to be worried when they told him that if a man didn't have sex, he could go mad! One evening the temptation and his loneliness was too much for him. He went out to a bar with these friends, and afterwards finished up sleeping with a prostitute. The next day he felt awful about it and resolved never to do this again.

At the end of the course Didier returned to his family and settled down with his family again. Two more years passed and now they had five children with a sixth on the way. When he began to feel unwell, he had almost forgotten about sleeping with the prostitute. At first he was just generally tired and started losing weight. Then he started having strange rashes and also frequent diarrhoea. So he went to the doctor. Who examined him and gave him various blood tests. Finally the doctor called him into his office and broke the sad news that he was HIV positive. He told him that he might already have infected his wife and even the youngest child.

One of the hospital workers heard about this, and told a member of Mary's family. Immediately her father came round to tell her to leave Didier and come back home. Mary refused to do this, but the pressure from her family made the whole situation worse.

Mary went to the hospital for the HIV test and found out that, indeed, she was HIV positive but none of her children were infected. They told her that if she took some special medicine during the rest of her pregnancy, the baby was less likely to be born HIV positive. Mary faithfully went to the hospital for these medicines and the baby was born healthy. However, Mary began to feel sick herself. Didier and Mary were in despair as they thought of the future of their six children. They were afraid to tell anyone of their problem in case people would start to avoid them. Soon though the problem was too big for them to bear, and they told their pastor.

Peter's and Ruth's Story

Pastor Peter and his wife Ruth lived in the capital city of a country where there was much fighting going on. One day Peter was out visiting some church members and his wife was at home with the children. Suddenly some rebel soldiers started coming into the town. They roamed around the streets, shooting people and raping women. Many of them were drunk or drugged. Before Ruth realized what was happening, they had broken into her compound. They grabbed her and one of the soldiers raped her, right there in front of the children. Then there was a loud explosion further down the street, and all the soldiers rushed out to see what was happening. Ruth and the children hid in one of the inner rooms.

Peter was trapped by the fighting in another part of the town, and wasn't able to get home until the next day. As soon as he arrived home and saw his wife, he knew something bad had happened but she found it very difficult to tell him about the rape. In the end, his oldest son told him. The whole family spent some hours crying and praying together. Peter and Ruth knew very well about the dangers of HIV and this was part of their pain.

The rebels left the town and things were calm again, though everyone knew it was a fragile peace. As Peter visited his church members, he found some other women who had been raped in the same way as his wife. Ruth was a brave committed Christian, and she decided to gather these women together so that they could help each other. Peter found a doctor to come and talk to them, and from him they learned that if they had come to him immediately after the rape, they could have taken a medicine to counteract the HIV virus. It was too late for that. Now they would have to wait three months before having an HIV test. Before then the results would not be sure. Another test would be repeated after six months. They also discussed how to protect their husbands from contracting HIV if in fact they had it. The doctor told them about condoms and how the husbands should use these all the time.

After three months these women went together for an HIV test. When the results came, there was pain and happiness as some were an HIV positive and some were not. They continued to meet together and help each other. Some of the husbands were finding it very difficult to accept what had happened so Peter and some other church leaders arranged a special seminar for the couples to help them accept the situation and receive comfort and courage from the Bible.

Discussion Question

1. *In your area, do people tell others if they know they have HIV or AIDS? Why or why not?*
2. *If they do not tell, how do you know when someone has AIDS?*
3. *How do people in your community treat people with HIV or AIDS?*

2. What Do You Know about HIV/AIDS?

Try this quiz. The answers are at the end of the chapter.

1. What does AIDS stand for?
2. What does HIV stand for?
3. What is the most frequent way that people worldwide are infected with HIV?
4. What is the second most frequent way?
5. Is there a cure for AIDS?
6. Is it possible for you to be infected by HIV by doing the following? Mark each one yes or no.
   a. Shaking hands with someone infected by HIV.
   b. Receiving an injection.
   c. Sharing food from the same bowl with someone with HIV.
   d. Using the same toilet as someone who has HIV.
   e. Using a razor blade that has been already used by another person.
   f. Having sex with someone who has HIV.
   g. Hugging a person with AIDS.
7. Can you tell by looking that someone has HIV?
8. What is the only way to tell for sure if you have HIV?

3. What Are Some False Beliefs That Increase the Spread of HIV?

Some people believe things that are not true about sex and HIV/AIDS. These lies keep them from protecting themselves from HIV/AIDS. Here are some of them:

- A man who does not have sex for some time will go mad or become impotent. Or young people need sex to develop normally. Or having sex will help a man get over an illness. These things are not true. Men do not need to have sex to develop normally, recover from illness, be sane, or remain fertile. Jesus and Paul were both celibate. (1 Cor 10:13, Gal 5:16-19)

- A woman should prove she is fertile before marriage. In the Bible, all sexual relations outside marriage are considered sexual immorality, and sexual immorality is sin (Gal 5:19). Children are a blessing, but they are not necessary for a Christian marriage (Gen 2:18).

- If Satan tempts you to sexual sin, you can't resist. The Bible says, "Resist the Devil and he will flee from you" (Ja 4:7). God will always give you a way to escape temptation. 1 Corinthians 10:13 says, "Every test that you have experienced is the kind that normally comes to people. But God keeps his promise, and he will not allow you to be tested beyond your power to remain firm; at the time you are put to the test, he will give you the strength to endure it, and so provide you with a way out."

- AIDS is a curse from God or it is caused by witchcraft. There is no mystery about how a person contracts it. It is spread through contact with blood or certain body fluids.

- A person who tells you that you have HIV/AIDS is cursing you, so it is better not to tell someone they have it. This results in the person giving it to others without even knowing it. President Museveni of Uganda said Africans should deal with HIV like they react when a lion is stalking the village. They should cry out and warn the villagers about the danger. No-one would keep quiet about a lion coming!

✱ DISCUSSION QUESTION

What are some other things that people believe in your area about the spread of HIV? Get someone who is medically trained, such as a doctor or dispensary nurse, to help you and your people know if these are true.

4. What Are Some Practices that Increase the Spread of AIDS?

Some cultures have customs or rituals that favour the spread of AIDS. Here are some:

- Levirate marriage (for example, a man may be obliged to marry the widow of his dead brother.) If the dead brother died of AIDS, the widow will possibly bring HIV into her new family.
- The low status of women which denies them the freedom to make choices about their sexuality and reproductive health.
- Funeral practices that involve contact with the body fluids of the dead person.
- Sharing needles for injections with others.
- Circumcision.

❋ DISCUSSION QUESTION

Are there practices in your area that increase the spread of HIV/AIDS? What are they?
What can we do about these things?

5. How Can We Teach Children about Sex and HIV/AIDS?

❋ DISCUSSION QUESTION

How do children learn about sex? Who teaches them? At what age does this take place?

The most likely way a young person will get infected with HIV is through sexual activity. The church needs to help those who teach children about sex know the facts about HIV/AIDS. Sex and HIV/AIDS education needs to start by the age of ten, or earlier if they ask questions. This education should be given before they become sexually active. Some very good books are available to teach children about sex and about HIV/AIDS. These could be translated into your language.

Having many sexual partners increases the chances of getting AIDS and is displeasing to God. Non-Christian agencies promote the use of condoms as a way to avoid contracting HIV. Condoms reduce the probability of getting HIV/AIDS, but abstinence before marriage is the only completely safe way to avoid getting it. It also

65

follows the Biblical teaching of reserving sex for marriage. The Bible also warns against incest (1 Cor 5:1). This teaching may challenge your traditional sexual practices. Young people will need a lot of encouragement to remain pure in this area. The example of the adults will speak louder than any teaching that is given.

Youth have a lot of energy. They need to be involved in good activities. If the church involves them in caring for people with AIDS, there can be many benefits.

- It makes them feel wanted and needed by the church.
- It helps them see the dangers of getting HIV/AIDS.
- It gives them something good to do so that they are not so likely to do bad things.

Youth can develop ways to teach HIV/AIDS awareness to others, through drama, song, presentations, or Bible study. They can visit the sick and read Scripture to them. They can do practical things to help them, like bringing water or food.

✿ SMALLL GROUPS DISCUSSION

1. *Are there any activities in your church that are useful and enjoyable for young people (10-20 years)?*

2. *What can your church do to help parents (or other appropriate people) teach young people about HIV/AIDS and sex?*

3. *How could young people in your church be involved in helping others avoid HIV/AIDS or in ministering to those who have it?*

6. How Can the Church Help a Person with HIV/AIDS?

Churches need to train a group of helpers to minister to those with AIDS (Mt 25: 34-36). Often these helpers go out two by two. AIDS victims need help in all areas of their lives.

A. Tell them about Jesus and the Bible.

Helpers should read Scripture, pray and sing with the sick person and his family. If the sick person is a Christian, he will receive much comfort from hearing about heaven. If the sick person is not a Christian, often he is open to hearing about how his sins can be forgiven, and how he can be sure he is going to heaven.

As the sick person begins to trust the helper, he can tell them how he is feeling about life and his illness. It is also important that the sick person knows he can tell God exactly how he feels. Psalm 38, where David expresses his real feelings to God when he was sick, might provide a model for AIDS victims. AIDS victims may want to write their own laments (See Lesson 2, Section 3b).

B. Help them tell others about their illness.

Often people want to hide that they are HIV positive. This does not help the sick person or the community as a whole. If they do not tell the real reason they are sick, people may wrongly accuse others of having caused the illness through a curse or witchcraft. It takes a brave person to be the first to say publicly that they have AIDS, but this can help others to do so. It is a very necessary step in helping the community "trap the lion."

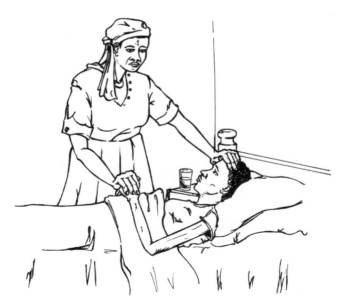

Everyone needs to know how HIV/AIDS is spread. It is equally important that they also know they will not catch HIV/AIDS by touching a sick person, or eating with them, or taking care of their needs.

C. They should not be excluded from their families or friends.

People need other people! AIDS victims may be rejected by their friends and even their family. The church needs to work with the community to help them accept these sick people and not be scared of them. Those who are suffering from AIDS can help each other by meeting together and sharing their experiences. The church could help to arrange this.

D. Help them understand the grief process.

It comes as a tremendous shock to someone to know that they are going to die. When someone has a fatal disease, they often go through stages that are similar to those that happen when we grieve: anger and denial, depression, and then acceptance. People who help these sick people need to know that it is normal to be angry at first. They may also deny that they have AIDS. A state of depression is also normal, and it may be some months before they can accept they are going to die. They may bargain with God, promising certain behaviours in exchange for their health. A good helper will be patient with them as they go through these stages.

E. Care for their bodies.

Two people may become HIV positive. One may live for six years, another may live for six months. This is partly due to the overall physical well-being of the person, but it is also due to his attitude, and the care he receives. People who have something to do will live longer than those who do nothing, so it is good to give AIDS victims some activity to help the family. They could learn to sew clothes or raise animals or engage in another activity that does not require great physical strength. In addition, good regular food will help the person to fight off disease. It is particularly important that the sick person eats plenty of fruit and vegetables so that they get good vitamins to keep their bodies healthy. They will need a lot of rest, and they should not smoke, or drink much alcohol. In some places, anti-viral drugs may be available that will help. If so, they need to follow the doctor's instructions exactly about taking them. If not they will do more harm than good.

The church also needs to arrange care of orphans whose parents have died of AIDS, and help widows and widowers who may themselves be HIV positive (Ja 1:27). The church should also help prostitutes find other ways to make a living.

CLOSING EXERCISE

1. *Do you have trained people to visit the sick, or is the pastor expected to do this alone?*

2. *Are all of the five areas listed above covered when you visit the sick? If not, how can you change this?*

3. *Study 1 Corinthians 6:13b-20. Why should a Christian flee from sexual immorality?*

4. *Read the following verses. What do they teach about visiting the sick?*

   2 Corinthians 1:3-5   *2 Corinthians 5:19-20*
   1 Corinthians 13:3-8   *Matthew 25:35-40*

5. *What is the one thing you would like to start doing in your church after reading this lesson?*

Answers to the Quiz

1. Acquired Immune Deficiency Syndrome
2. Human Immunodeficiency Virus
3. Through unprotected sex
4. By mother to child transmission
5. No
6. a. No, b. Yes, c. No, d. No, e. Yes, f. Yes, g. No,
7. No
8. Blood test in a laboratory

Lesson 7

CARING FOR THE CAREGIVER

1. The Overloaded Pastor

Pastor Bamba has been working very hard since the war broke out between his people and a neighbouring ethnic group. He was out of the country during those weeks but since he returned he has heard story after story about what happened. As the pastor to his people he has felt he should always be ready to listen, especially since he was not there at the time of the conflict. He has been back with his people now for five months.

Two months ago his best friend came to him. He recounted in detail the ordeal of seeing his wife and children killed in front of him during the fighting. Ever since then, Bamba can't get the images of what his friend told him out of his mind. His wife has noticed that he has not been sleeping well for the last few weeks and awakens with the slightest noise. He has noticed that he no longer has the energy he used to have and wakes up feeling tired. Three times in the past month he has awakened in the middle of the night after a frightening nightmare in which people from the neighbouring ethnic group are chasing him.

For the past month he has felt more and more discouraged. He no longer wants to preach and has been thinking of resigning. He feels he has been a failure as a pastor. His wife is worried because he rarely talks to her any more. Last week, while bicycling to a neighbouring village, he ran his bike off the road, broke his arm and ruined the bike.

1. *Why do you think Pastor Bamba is having all these problems?*

2. *Do you know any people who have become so overloaded helping others that they became very discouraged or sick? What do they say? How do they behave?*

2. How Can We Know If a Caregiver Is Overloaded?

Taking care of other people can wear us out. We can get so busy caring for others that we do not take time to care for ourselves. If we behave in some of the following ways, we may be overloaded:

- Feeling angry or sad all the time.
- Feeling tired and irritable.
- Not sleeping well.
- Having problems with relationships.
- Questioning the truth of our faith.
- Questioning God's goodness and power.
- Beginning to believe the lies of Satan.
- Becoming ill or having many accidents.
- Resenting those who need our help.

If we have some of these symptoms for a long time, we need to change something in our situation. If we allow ourselves to become exhausted, we will not be able to carry on with the work God has given us.

✸ Small Group Discussion

Have you ever felt overloaded? Describe how you felt.

3. Why Is It Difficult To Be a Caregiver?

In times of war or crisis, many people have problems and need to talk to someone about them, so a pastor's work increases. He may face some of the following difficulties.

A. A caregiver may have too many people to care for.

A caregiver may think he or she is indispensable to God's work and has to personally care for everyone. Or church members may think that the pastor has to do everything. They may want to talk to him and no one else.

B. A caregiver can be the object of people's anger.

People who have experienced trauma are often angry. They can sometimes lash out without reason at the people around them. This can include the caregivers, even though they are only trying to help. When this happens, the caregiver must recognize that the hurt person is not really angry with him. He must not take it personally.

C. A caregiver may be manipulated by people.

Some people who come with problems are not really wanting solutions. They want to blame others, but are not willing to change themselves. If the caregiver tries to confront them about their part in the problem, they might try to change the subject. These people can take up a lot of time. Caregivers need to discern those that really want help from those who are merely seeking attention.

D. A caregiver may find out certain things in confidence that he must tell others.

When people share their problems with a caregiver, what they say is held in confidence. Some things, however, cannot be kept secret. These would include illegal activities, rape, plans that would hurt someone, or plans of suicide. Those speaking to the caregiver need to understand ahead of time that these things must be reported to the authorities.

E. A caregiver may find that he enjoys being at the centre of everything.

The caregiver may enjoy a sense of power over other people's lives. It may make him feel needed when otherwise he is lacking in confidence. Sometimes helping others is a way of avoiding looking at one's own problems. These are not good reasons for helping others. The caregiver may need to stop and look at his own motivation for helping others before God to be sure they are pure.

F. A caregiver may ignore how he really feels inside.

The caregiver may think he should be strong enough to bear heavy burdens without complaining or becoming angry. But if he denies his own feelings of anger and sadness and fear, he runs the risk of serious spiritual and emotional exhaustion.

G. A caregiver may neglect his own family.

Caring for people takes lots of time. A caregiver can easily spend so much time with others that his own wife and children are neglected. This will eventually cause serious problems. His wife may become depressed or angry. The children may feel angry that their father has time for everyone else but has no time for them. He may no longer be at home enough to discipline them. The relationship between the man and his wife and children may become distant, leaving the father feeling lonely in his own home.

SMALL GROUP DISCUSSION

What difficulties have you experienced as you have cared for people?

4. How Can Caregivers Take Care of Themselves?

(Hold up a machete and sharpening file.) What will happen to this machete if I never sharpen it? Is the time I take to sharpen it wasted or well-used?

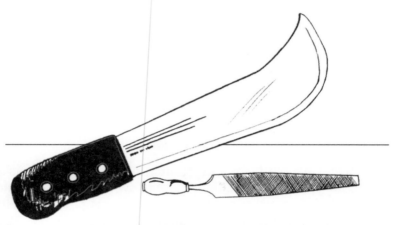

Taking Time to Sharpen the Machete

We are God's instruments for good in the world (2 Tim 2:21). If instruments are not cared for, they will break down and lose their usefulness. Just as we must stop using a machete to clean it and sharpen it, so we must stop and care for ourselves. Then we will be able to take care of others.

When we listen to people's problems, we absorb some of their pain and carry it with us. When we listen to many people, the burden of all their pain can be very heavy, much heavier than any one of them bears individually. We have to be careful not to be crushed by it. (Ps 103:13-14)

A. Let God care for you.

✤ SMALL GROUP EXERCISE:

    1. Read I Kings 19:3-8. What did God do for Elijah when he was tired and discouraged?

    2. Read Mark 6:30-32. What did Jesus tell the disciples after they had finished ministering to many people?

God has promised to comfort us, help us and be strong for us when we are overwhelmed. He understands that we are weak. Even Jesus got tired and sad and felt troubled. The Bible gives us many examples of God's servants who were so tired that they could not continue their work. God gave them special care at that time. Take time in prayer to know God's love and care for you (Ps 35:27).

B. Share your burdens with others.

Have regular times for sharing and prayer with a small group or another person. Share with other caregivers or mature Christians. In the same way that people who have experienced trauma need to talk it out, caregivers need to share their burdens with someone (Gal 6:2).

C. Share the workload with others.

🌸 DISCUSSION QUESTION

Read Exodus 18:13-23. What was Moses' problem? How did he solve it?

Sharing the workload means first of all, giving up some of the control of your ministry. Others will do things differently than you do, and you will no longer be at the centre of everything that happens.

Identify others in the church who are mature and who are gifted in helping others. It is good to have a balanced team of people: men and women, from different ages and ethnic groups (Rom 12:4-8). Train them how to help others. By doing this, you help people respect their ability to help others. Your satisfaction then comes from training them well and seeing them succeed.

If people from other churches are coming to you, explain what is happening to their pastors or priests so that they don't think that you are trying to steal their members from them. Train these pastors and priests in how to help people with wounded hearts.

Help church members understand that people besides the pastor can help them. In some religions only the priest can do the work, but in Christianity, church members can minister to one another. Help church members understand that you will be able to work better if you can take time to "sharpen your machete."

D. Take time away from the situation.

Find opportunities to rest and get away from the difficulties and pain. Jesus and his disciples did. "There were so many people coming and going that Jesus and his disciples didn't even have time to eat. So he said to them, 'Let us go off by ourselves to some place where we will be alone and you can rest a while'" (Mk 6:31). Sometimes it takes several days of rest to begin to release the burden.

Spouses and children are part of the ministry God gives us. They are not a barrier to it. Caregivers need to reserve time for their wife and children. In some cases, a family retreat or holiday might be appropriate.

E. *Take care of your physical body.*

- Get exercise daily. Exercise releases stress.

- Get enough sleep. Adults need 7-8 hours per night.

- Eat a good, nourishing diet. Inexpensive peanuts, eggs, grains, fruits and vegetables are available in most places, even if money for food is limited. Don't become so busy with the work that you forget to eat. You need good food to be strong physically.

CLOSING EXERCISE

Read Psalm 1 together. Discuss what is needed for trees to grow and bare fruits. What ways does God want to give us these things? How can we receive these from Him?

In small groups, describe your workload. How can you care for yourself and your family as you care for others?

Lesson 8

Response:
TAKING YOUR PAIN TO THE CROSS

PREPARING FOR THIS EXERCISE

Instructions for Leaders

This exercise should be done towards the end of the seminar, after people have been thinking about their heart wounds and feel ready to share their pain with God and others. It must be done in a way that people know that they will not be criticized, and that what they share will not be used against them. It is not a magic ritual, but a way to experience God beginning to heal our pain. It is often done as an evening session.

To prepare for this exercise, the leaders need to make a cross out of wood and get paper and pens for everyone. They will also need matches and a place outside to burn the papers. It is very important that the papers burn without a lot of difficulty, as that would distract from the meaning of the experience.

If it's not possible to make a cross, the leaders need to devise some other symbol of the cross. A cross drawn on a box could suffice. If paper is not available, or if people are not literate, other items that can burn, like small sticks, could be used to symbolize their pain. This might also be necessary in areas where people are afraid their security might be at risk if these things were written down even for a moment.

If the papers are to be nailed to the cross, leaders will need to have a hammer and nails. If the papers are to be put in a box at the foot of the cross, they'll need a box that is ready for this.

The large group will be divided into small groups of three during the exercise for a time of sharing their deepest pain. The leaders will need to decide in advance how best to divide up the group. Sometimes, it is important to keep men with men, pastors with pastors, and women with women. If the point of the seminar is ethnic reconciliation, people from different ethnic groups should be put together. When people trust each other enough to share their deepest pain, and when they hear each other's pain, healing takes place. Children should be grouped with at least one adult. In some situations, leaders may allow participants to choose who they meet with.

It may be good to talk about the experience the next day, to discuss how people felt about it, and how they could do this with other groups in their churches. Healing takes time. This ceremony can be an important part of the process of healing. It will not necessarily heal all hurts instantaneously.

1. Identify the Wounds of Your Heart

We are here to take our pain to the cross. We are taught in Scripture that Jesus not only came to bear our sins, but also to bear our pain. Isaiah 53:3-4 says, "We despised him and rejected him; he endured suffering and pain.... Surely he took up our infirmities and carried our sorrows, yet we considered him stricken by God, smitten by him, and afflicted."

Isaiah 61:1-3 says,

> The Sovereign LORD has filled me with his Spirit.
> He has chosen me and sent me
> To bring good news to the poor,
> To heal the broken-hearted,
> To announce release to captives
> And freedom to those in prison.
> He has sent me to proclaim
> That the time has come
> When the LORD will save his people
> And defeat their enemies.
> He has sent me to comfort all who mourn,

To give to those who mourn in Zion
Joy and gladness instead of grief,
A song of praise instead of sorrow.
They will be like trees
That the LORD himself has planted.
They will all do what is right,
And God will be praised for what he has done.

Jesus felt the full burden of human pain and sinfulness. Jesus knows the pain that is in our hearts and we need to bring it to him so he can heal us. In this exercise, we will experience bringing our pains to the cross.

A. Write down your worst pain.

Ask God to show you the painful things that are buried deep in your heart. Which are the ones that are most painful? Which memories do you not like to think about? Write these down. We will bring these to the cross and burn them later, so no one will ever see what you have written.

Be as specific as possible. You should write down the worst things that you remember such as:

- Bad things that have been done to you.

- Bad things you have seen done to others, or bad dreams you have had.

- Bad things you have heard about that have happened to others.

- Bad things that you may have done to others.

This should take about twenty minutes. It is helpful for people to be alone as they do this.

B. Share your pain in small groups.

Divide into groups of three. Each person may share something they have written down. The other two should listen without criticizing or offering advice. Share openly but don't dwell on the violent parts unnecessarily. Be sure all three have an opportunity to share.

If someone is not able to write, they could make a mark on paper, or have someone else write for them, or use a stick to represent their pain. At the end decide what things the group would like to share with the large group. Take about thirty minutes for this.

C. The small groups share with the large group.

In the large group, some people may share briefly the pain that they have experienced. Be specific, but do not tell the whole story again. For example, you might say, "I saw my father being killed" or "soldiers pointed a gun at my head and were ready to shoot me."

When everyone who wants to share has done so, the leader asks, "What can we do with these pains?" Then he reads Isaiah 53:4-6:

> But he endured the suffering that should have been ours,
> the pain that we should have borne.
> All the while we thought that his suffering
> was punishment sent by God.
> But because of our sins he was wounded,
> beaten because of the evil we did.
> We are healed by the punishment he suffered,
> made whole by the blows he received.
> All of us were like sheep that were lost,
> each of us going his own way.
> But the LORD made the punishment fall on him,
> the punishment all of us deserved.

2. Bring Your Wounds and Pain to Jesus

A. Talk to Jesus about your pain.

Take some time to bring your pain to Jesus. Tell him exactly what it is: for example, anger, sadness, loneliness, or feeling abandoned. Empty your soul. Let any emotions you feel about the pain come out.

B. Bring your pain to the cross.

Bring the paper on which you wrote your pain to the cross. Nail it to the cross, or put it in the box at the foot of the cross. As you do, say, "I'm handing over my suffering to Jesus who died on the cross for me."

C. Burn the papers.

When all the papers have been deposited, take them outside and burn them. This shows that the suffering we have experienced has become like ashes (Isa 61:3). This is a stage in knowing God's healing.

Afterwards, each person should pray for the person on either side of them that Jesus will continue to heal their wounded hearts.

3. Share the Good Things God Has Done

Invite some people to share the ways that they have seen God at work, even in the midst of their problems.

Thank God and praise him in words and songs because he is healing the wounds in our hearts.

Lesson 9

HOW CAN WE FORGIVE OTHERS?

1. Real and Fake Forgiveness

Act out the following short skits:

1. Taku is sitting with his friend, Bru. He says, "Last week Samuel really hurt me. Right in front of all the other pastors he said I was no good at preaching sermons. My heart still hurts about this." After Bru leaves, Samuel walks in. Samuel says, "Please forgive me for what I said last week." Then Taku says, "There is nothing to forgive, I didn't mind."

2. Pastor Job is talking to Nguesan, a church member. Nguesan says, "I've tried to forgive my father for being cruel to me when I was a child, but it is hard." Pastor Job says, "Well you must forget all about that. Until you forget, you can't say you have forgiven him."

3. Lambo taught the adult Bible class last Sunday in the place of the regular teacher. A member of the class, Silas, made a big fuss about a minor point Lambo taught and argued a lot about it. Later that week, when the regular teacher thanked him, Lambo said, "I never want to teach that class again!" He told the teacher what had happened and how Silas had embarrassed him. The teacher offered to go with Lambo to discuss with Silas. When they did so, Lambo expressed his dismay at the argument in class, his frustration at not being able to answer well enough, and his embarrassment. Silas apologized and asked his forgiveness, which Lambo was eager to give.

Which of these situations show real forgiveness? How is it different from the others?

2. Forgiveness Is Not . . .

* saying the offence didn't matter.
* saying we were not hurt by what the person did (Eph 4:25).
* acting as if the event never happened.
* dependent on the offender apologizing first or changing their behaviour (Rom 5:8).
* letting the person who did wrong avoid the consequences of their action (Rom 13:2).
* letting the offender hurt us or other innocent people again.
* trusting a person again right after they hurt us.

3. What Is Forgiveness?

A. Forgiveness involves bringing the pain to Christ.

Forgiving someone means that we recognize that the person has wronged us, and we accept the pain their sin has caused us. We bring our pain to the cross and release it to Jesus. When Jesus heals our pain, then we will be able to forgive those who have hurt us. If we think forgiving is too hard for us to do, we are right. God is the only one who can enable us to forgive. (Mt 11:28-30)

B. Complete forgiveness of a deep hurt takes time.

Forgiveness does not happen all at once. It is like a journey where we lose our way repeatedly. We start to forgive, but then we circle back as we remember the hurt of the offence. Then we forgive again a little more thoroughly, and gradually we make our way to complete forgiveness.

When we forgive someone, we will still remember what happened. At first, we may still feel the pain associated with it. When this happens, we need to continue to take the parts that hurt to Jesus. The commitment to forgive often comes before the feelings of forgiveness, and sometimes long before. As we bring our hurt to Jesus over and over, eventually we will feel less pain when we remember the event. Then we can know that our forgiveness is complete. (1 Pt 2:21-25)

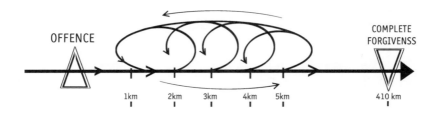

The Cycle of Forgiveness

To forgive someone does not mean that we trust them immediately. Just because we have forgiven a person does not mean that he has changed. Even if he has changed, our trust in him is broken and will take time to rebuild. Little by little as we have good experiences with that person, we will begin to trust them again. But it may take a long time before we can trust him completely, if ever.

C. Forgiveness does not depend on what the other person does.

Often we are unwilling to forgive until the offender has apologized to us. Or we want to see that the person has changed their behaviour before we forgive them. Like Jesus, we need to forgive people, even if they are not sorry about the evil they have done. On the cross he said, "Forgive them, Father! They don't know what they are doing" (Lk 23:34).

D. Forgiveness does not release the offender from facing the consequences of their act.

Forgiving someone does not mean that they will not be punished if they have done wrong things. By forgiving, we allow God to judge and take revenge (Rom 12:19-21). He can do this much better than we can. God has also given national and traditional leaders the job of punishing criminals and protecting the innocent (Rom 13:1-4). Even though we have forgiven someone, it may be necessary to bring them to justice, for the good of society.

Even though we have forgiven our enemies, we should defend the innocent from violent or evil people if they try to harm them again.

Forgiveness also requires the offender to pay back what he has taken, if possible. Some things, like a woman's virginity or a person's life, can never really be repaid. But if someone has stolen chickens, he should pay them back (Num 5:5-7). Sin must be paid for, even if it involves great expense. God gave us the model to follow when Jesus paid for the sins of the whole world on the cross, (and he was completely innocent). (Is 53:5)

❀ DISCUSSION QUESTION

How are the biblical ideas about forgiveness similar to our traditional ones? How are they different?

4. Why Does God Want Us to Forgive Other People?

A. Forgiveness frees us from anger and bitterness.

If we do not forgive someone who has offended us, we are the ones who suffer. Our anger allows Satan a way into our hearts (Eph 4:26-27; 2 Cor 2:10-11). We become slaves of our anger and bitterness, and they begin to destroy us. Refusing to forgive can make us physically ill with headaches, stomach ulcers, or heart problems. It may make us become as violent and evil as those who offended us. Forgiveness releases us from all this. We forgive for our own good.

Forgiveness Sets Us Free from the Chains of Bitterness

If we do not forgive others, we pass our hatred on to our children. This can result in cycles of revenge and violence between groups which can go on for generations. Only forgiveness can break the cycle. Forgiveness also allows us to begin the healing process. (Rom 4:6-8, Heb 12:14-15))

B. Forgiveness allows us to receive God's forgiveness.

God's forgiveness depends on our forgiving those who offend us. Matthew 6:14-15 says, "If you forgive others the wrongs they have done to you, your Father in heaven will also forgive you. But if you do not forgive others, then your Father will not forgive the wrongs you have done." (See also Mk 11:25.)

C. Forgiveness shows that we understand Christ's sacrifice and our salvation.

When we understand how much we have offended God by our sinfulness, and how Jesus forgave us even before we repented (1 Jn 4:10), any offence we have experienced will seem small. We will want to extend that same forgiveness to others (Eph 4:32; Mt 18:21-35).

D. Forgiveness allows us to be reconciled with those who have offended us.

Until we forgive those who have offended us, our relationship with them will suffer. Forgiveness makes it possible for our relationship with them to be restored. Full restoration, however, requires repentance and forgiveness on both sides.

E. Forgiveness can change the person who offended us.

Forgiving someone may be the start of God bringing that person to repent. In Acts 7, as Stephen was dying, he forgave those who were killing him. One of those people was Saul, who later became Paul the apostle (Acts 7:60-8:1).

Small Group Discussion

1. *What do you find the hardest thing about forgiving someone? What has helped you the most to forgive others?*
2. *What traditions do we have that help us to repent and forgive others? What traditions do we have that hinder us from repenting and forgiving?*

5. What If We Are the Ones Who Have Caused the Offence?

A. How do we repent?

- We allow God's spirit to show us how much our sin hurts him and others. This may make us sad and even weep as God breaks our hearts (Ja 4:8-9). This sorrow can be good for us. "For God can use sorrow in our lives to help us turn away from sin and seek salvation. We will never regret that kind of sorrow. But sorrow without repentance is the kind that results in death" (2 Cor 7:10 NLT). Both Peter and Judas were sad that they had denied Jesus, but Peter's sorrow brought him closer to God; Judas' led him to kill himself.

- We take responsibility for what we have done and clearly state our sin (Prov 28:13; Ps 32:3-5).

- We ask God to forgive us for the sin, and then accept that he has done so (1 Jn 1:9).

- We ask those we have offended to forgive us, without defending ourselves or blaming them (Ja 5:16). We should ask forgiveness in such a way that all those affected by our sin are aware of our repentance. For example, if we have insulted someone in front of others, then we should ask forgiveness in front of the other people as well.

- If we have repented in our hearts, we will show it by the way we act (Acts 26:20b).

- Repentance may involve paying back what was taken (Num 5:5-7).

B. How can the church help people repent?

Church leaders are charged to watch over the spiritual life of their members (1 Pet 5:2-3). If a member is sinning, and will not listen to those who talk to him about his sin, the church leaders should talk to him (Mt 18:15-17; Gal 6:1).

If the person refuses to repent even after repeated efforts, he must be excluded from the church (1 Cor 5:4-5,11). This is a very painful process. It is done to protect the church's purity (1 Cor 5:6-7), and to bring the person to repentance. Even after he is excluded from the group, the leaders should continue to try to help him to come to repentance.

✿ DISCUSSION QUESTION

As a church, how do we deal with members when they sin? Has this helped them to repent?

CLOSING EXERCISES

Omit these exercises if the group will be going on to the final ceremony.

1. *Have one person read each of the following verses aloud and give the main point.*

   Ephesians 4:32   Matthew 18:21-22

   Matthew 18:35   Romans 12:14

2. *Take five minutes in silence to ask God to show you any sins that you need to repent of. Confess those sins to God and receive his forgiveness. At the end of the time, read 1 John 1:9 aloud.*

3. *Take another five minutes to reflect on any people that you need to forgive. Ask God to help you forgive them.*

4. *Share together what God has shown you about forgiveness.*

5. *Praise God, in words and in song, that he forgives us and enables us to forgive others.*

HOW CAN WE LIVE AS CHRISTIANS IN THE MIDST OF CONFLICT?

Use this lesson if you have ethnic tension in your area. Use it after the lesson on forgiveness, and before the final ceremony.

1. Liwi-Oki Conflict

In the country of Bingola, two ethnic groups – the Liwis and the Okis – had been fighting over one area of land which both groups claimed. This fighting had been going on for over a hundred years. Nearly every family had a member who had been killed or injured by the opposite group. Mothers and fathers taught their children from an early age how dangerous and savage the other group was. All the schools were either for Liwi children or for Oki children. They never mixed together.

Jonah Nga was a Liwi teacher, and he was also a real Christian. As part of a development committee, he was elected to go to a meeting with an international NGO (not a Christian organization) in the capital. Bozon was an Oki and had been a pastor for some years of a small Baptist church. He was also chosen to go to the same meeting of the NGO.

There were twenty-five people from Bingola in the meeting – four of the group were Liwi, five were Oki. Each group sat as far away from the other as possible, making very sure never to sit next to one of the other group. As far as possible they tried to pretend the other people were not there. After two days Jonah and Bozon were asked to serve on a small sub-committee of four members. At the beginning, Bozon and Jonah wouldn't talk to each other directly but, as the meeting went on, they got more interested in the subject they were discussing, and started to interact with each other.

At the end of the meeting, Jonah and Bozon went on talking and discovered they were both Christians! To start with, both of them thought in their hearts, "Can a Liwi/Oki be a real Christian?" Once they were able to accept that startling fact, they began to discuss how they could help bring reconciliation to their groups. But first they had to express many things they had heard as children. Bozon asked Jonah, "Do Liwis really eat old people when they are too old to work?" Jonah laughed at that, but in return asked Bozon, "Do Okis always go to bed with a spear in their hand?" Soon they discovered that many of the stories they had been told weren't true at all.

✻ SMALL GROUP DISCUSSION

1. *Why did Bozon and Jonah find it hard to accept that the other one was a Christian?*

2. *What are the other Liwis and Okis going to think and do when they see Bozon and Jonah talking together?*

3. *How could they begin to bring the two groups together?*

2. What Are Some Causes of Conflict between Groups?

A. Desire for resources

At the base of every conflict is the desire to have something so strongly we are willing to fight for it (Ja 4:1-3). We may fight over land or water, for example. We may be greedy and want more than our share of the resources, or fearful that others will take what we have from us.

B. Ineffective or unjust governments

God has put governments in place to see that people receive justice (Rom 13:1-4). When governments do not do their job and there is widespread suffering, at some point people rebel. In times of political instability, old conflicts between groups re-surface because there is no one to stop them.

C. Trouble-makers

Some individuals, like Hitler, can single-handedly stir up whole nations to war. The newspapers and radio can also fan the flames of hatred. Soon people are killing each other without really understanding why, and the cycle of violence begins. Once it is started, it can only be stopped by radical forgiveness. (Rom 1:28-32)

D. A heritage of prejudice

Children inherit prejudice and hatred for other groups from their parents. Whenever we think, "The people from the other group are always...," we are expressing a prejudice. Prejudices portray all members of the other group as if they are the same, and all bad. Prejudices keep people from ever finding out what the other group is really like. If they did, they would discover that their prejudices are not accurate. There are both good and bad people in every group. (Acts 10:28-36)

In times of conflict, all the problems are blamed on the other group. To be able to kill them without feeling guilty, the other group is portrayed as if the people aren't even human.

Meanwhile, people see their own group as superior, and entitled to certain things, like land or status. For example, a group may feel entitled to special respect and service from a group that were their slaves earlier in history.

❋ DISCUSSION QUESTIONS

1. *Are there conflicts in your community or country? What are the roots of these conflicts?*

2. *What are the prejudices you may have inherited about another group? Can you think of any evidence that would show these ideas are not true?*

3. How do others describe your group? What evidence might they have for this description?

3. How Can We Live as Christians in the Midst of Conflict?

❀ DISCUSSION QUESTION

Why is it difficult to live as Christians in the midst of conflict?

God calls Christians to be salt and light, bringing the good news of Jesus Christ into evil and dark situations (Mt 5:13-16; Phil 2:14-16). Christians are to have their minds transformed by Christ. This means that they will react differently from non-Christians (Rom 12:1-2). This is the path of blessing, but it is not easy. It will need a daily, intentional decision.

A. God wants us to trust in His sovereignty.

Matthew 10:28-31 says, "Do not be afraid of those who kill the body but cannot kill the soul; rather be afraid of God, who can destroy both body and soul in hell. For only a penny you can buy two sparrows, yet not one sparrow falls to the ground without your Father's consent. As for you, even the hairs of your head have all been counted. So do not be afraid; you are worth much more than many sparrows!"

Not even a small bird dies without God knowing it. We can trust that God sees what happens to us. He will use it for our good (Rom 8:28).

Even when evil is done, it is within God's larger plan. We must look beyond the evildoer to see the hand of God in the situation. Both Joseph and Jesus suffered, but God used their suffering for good (Gen 45:5-7; Acts 3:13-15). God is at work, even through people's evil intentions.

God tells us that our lives are not our own. God knows the date of our death before we're even born (Ps 139:15-16). If we have been spared while others have died, it is because God still has a purpose for our lives (Esther 4:13-14; 2 Thes 1:11-12).

B. God wants us to be prepared to give up everything but Christ.

In times of conflict, everything that defined who we are may be taken from us: our family members, our homes, our possessions, our work, our own lives. Only Christ can never be taken from us. 1 Peter 1:3-6 says, "Let us give thanks to the God and Father of our Lord Jesus Christ! Because of his great mercy he gave us new life by raising Jesus Christ from death. This fills us with a living hope, and so we look forward to possessing the rich blessings that God keeps for his people. He keeps them for you in heaven, where they cannot decay or spoil or fade away. They are for you, who through faith are kept safe by God's power for the salvation which is ready to be revealed at the end of time."

We must voluntarily give up the cultural prejudices we grew up with. Old ways of judging others must go; they are worldly and cause divisions. 2 Corinthians 5:16-18 says, "No longer, then, do we judge anyone by human standards. Even if at one time we judged Christ according to human standards, we no longer do so. Anyone who is joined to Christ is a new being; the old is gone, the new has come. All this is done by God, who through Christ changed us from enemies into his friends and gave us the task of making others his friends also."

Our only desire must be to know Christ, and to help others know him (Gal 2:20; Phil 1:21; 3:8). Christ has redeemed us from all of the evil in our past (1 Pet 1:17-19).

We must give up any rights we think we might have as members of our group. God has no favourites; all people are accepted equally by him (Acts 10:34; Rom 2:9-11). We now belong to a new nation with other believers where everyone is equal (1 Pet 2:9; Eph 2:18-22; Rev 5:9-10). Christ provided the model for us to follow when he gave up his rights as God to save us (Phil 2:5-11).

Everything we give up for Christ will be rewarded one hundred times (Mt 19:29; Lk 9:23), but the process is not easy.

C. God tells us not to take revenge, but show love.

Romans 12:19-21 says, "Never take revenge, my friends, but instead let God's anger do it. For the scripture says, 'I will take revenge, I will pay back, says the Lord.' Instead, as the scripture says: 'If your enemies are hungry, feed them; if they are thirsty, give them a drink; for by doing this you will make them burn with shame.' Do not let evil defeat you; instead, conquer evil with good."

As Christians, we no longer have the responsibility to take revenge for the wrongs done to us or our families. We are to show love and allow God to punish others (Mt 5:38-42). Revenge does not bring peace to our hearts or bring back what was lost. It only perpetuates the violence.

Each human life is sacred because it reflects God's image (Gen 1:27). We are not to destroy or mistreat it, but we can defend our lives and the lives of others.

God works through governments to bring justice, punish evil doers, and protect the innocent. "Everyone must obey state authorities, because no authority exists without God's permission, and the existing authorities have been put there by God. Whoever opposes the existing authority opposes what God has ordered; and anyone who does so will bring judgment on himself.... They are God's servants and carry out God's punishment on those who do evil" (Rom 13:1-2.4b).

Even when governments are unjust and ineffective, we should not take the law into our own hands. The most powerful thing Jesus did was to make himself completely vulnerable to his enemies on the cross (1 Pet 2:21-23). People like Ghandi in India and Martin Luther King in the United States have challenged governments by standing against evil without using violence. These movements have resulted in correcting widespread injustice more effectively than a violent reaction could have, and those involved were not guilty of shedding blood.

D. God wants us to receive strength from Him.

In times of conflict, we need to stay close to God. We should read the Bible regularly (2 Tim 3:16-17; Rom 12:1-2). We need to spend time in prayer bringing our wounds and concerns to God, and receiving his peace in our hearts (Phil 4:6-7). Writing a lament about our experiences might help us to express our pain to God.

We may need to spend time away from the situation "on the mountain" with God to restore our souls (Mk 6:31, 45-46). The Holy Spirit will help us, even when we are weak (Acts 1:8; 2 Cor 12:9-10).

We need to meet with other Christians, share our pains, and pray for one another (Heb 10:25; Ja 5:16). We should be careful not to talk about the situation in ways that sow more seeds of bitterness (I Cor 14:26).

4. How Can We Help Bring Reconciliation?

 EXERCISE

Prepare a skit in which two groups go through the motions of reconciliation but are not really reconciled.

A. We can become a bridge between the groups in conflict.

God created us to be social beings. By nature, we want and need to belong to a group. In times of conflict, we may need to sacrifice that need to belong and become a bridge between the two groups in conflict. For example, we should share food and resources with those in need, no matter which side they are on. This may put our lives at risk. Our "enemies" may want to kill us because we are their enemies. But our brothers may also want to kill us because we have befriended the enemy. Close family members may condemn us. (Eph 2:11-22)

God calls us to love our enemies (Mt 5:43-48). When we do this, we no longer have any enemies. All people become our brothers.

If we do not know any other peace-makers in the situation, we may be alone with God as our only friend (Mt 5:9). We may well feel we are aliens in this world (1 Pet 1:1,2; Heb 11:13-16).

As a bridge between the two groups, we need to try to understand the pain that each side of the conflict has experienced from their perspective. Then we can help each side understand the pain of the other, to give up their prejudice and view them as humans. (Rom 12:17-21)

If we hear too much from one side and we begin to see only their point of view, we need to spend time with the other side to recover perspective.

B. We can lead people to Christ so that they find healing and repent of their sins.

God has given us the ministry of reconciling people to Christ (2 Cor 5:17-20). Where there is conflict, nearly everyone has wounds of the heart. These should be brought to Christ so he can heal the pain. Where people have sinned against others, they must repent and ask God and those they have hurt to forgive them.

C. We can help people repent of the sins of their group.

The worst things that happen in the world are caused not by individuals, but by groups: ethnic groups, governments, churches. Even if we were not involved personally in causing suffering, as members of our group, we need to repent before God for the suffering our group has caused. Then we need to ask forgiveness of those we have hurt on behalf of our group. In the Bible, Daniel, Nehemiah, and Ezra all did this on behalf of their people (Dan 9:4-9; Neh 9:2-36; Ezra 9:5-15; Lev 26:40). There are also many current examples of people doing this today: Americans asking forgiveness of Native Americans, Germans asking forgiveness of the Dutch for the suffering they inflicted on them during World War II, South African Whites asking forgiveness of Blacks. Usually, when one group repents and asks forgiveness, the other group repents as well, and reconciliation follows.

D. Groups should discuss their problems openly and find solutions.

When the pain in people's hearts is healed, then the real problems that started the conflict must be addressed. People need to work together, give and take, and find a solution that is fair and acceptable to all.

No problems are too small to need attention. No matter how small, they can become big if they are not solved.

E. Celebrate Christ and the unity he brings.

When Christ has broken down barriers between us, we need to celebrate and praise him together (Eph 2:14). He is Lord. He sets us free from the lies and traps of the enemy.

CLOSING EXERCISE

Read this story about ethnic tensions in the early church. Then act it out. Divide into three groups: the homeland Jews, the foreign Jews, and the apostles. The homeland Jews and the foreign Jews should present their case to the apostles in turn. Then the apostles can give their decision. Finally discuss the questions at the end of the story.

Over five hundred years before Jesus came, the powerful nations of Assyria, Babylon, and Persia conquered Israel. To keep Israel from becoming strong again, they took most of the people into exile to live in other countries. By the time Jesus was born, many Jews had lived outside their homeland for hundreds of years. They spoke Greek, the common language of the day, and lived like Greek people, but they were pious Jews who continued to worship the Lord God. They made trips to their homeland when they could, and believed it was good to be buried there. Older couples liked to move back to Israel so that when they died, they would be buried there. Often the husband died first, leaving his widow in need of someone to provide for her.

Meanwhile, the Jews who stayed in Israel through the years continued to speak their own language and practise their cultural traditions. Life was hard for them, but they persevered. And they felt that because they had never left their land or traditions, they were better in God's eyes. They looked down on the foreign Jews.

One of their traditions was to care for widows. The tithes that they offered to God were used to feed the Levites, aliens, fatherless and widows (Dt 26:12). None of the other cultures at the time took care of widows like the Jews in Israel did. Out of obedience to God, they took care of the foreign Jewish widows just like they took care of their own. There were so many foreign Jewish widows that the homeland Jews had a hard time caring for them.

In the early church, it wasn't long before the tensions between the homeland Jews and the foreign Jews became apparent. The foreign Jews complained that their widows were not being given their share when the food supplies were handed out each day (Acts 6:1-7). The apostles called a meeting to address the problem openly. They recognized that these ethnic tensions could destroy the church. So they had the group choose seven men to deal with the problem. At least one of these men, Nicolaus, was a foreign Jew from Antioch. They dealt with the problem, and the church continued to grow. The love between foreign Jewish Christians and homeland Jewish Christians was a strong testimony to those outside the church.

Over and over again, the differences between the foreign Jews and homeland Jews caused tensions in the church. Each time, the apostles took the initiative early on, discussed the problem openly, and worked out a solution that was acceptable to all (Acts 15, for example). And the church grew.

✻ DISCUSSION QUESTIONS

1. *What were the historical causes of the conflict in Acts 6:1-7?*
2. *How did the church leaders keep the ethnic tensions from ruining the church?*
3. *Do you have ethnic tensions in your own church? Discuss the causes and possible solutions.*
4. *Acknowledge any prejudices your group may have. Pray and ask God to deliver you from them.*
5. *Pray for your enemies (1 Pet 4:8).*

Lesson 11

LOOKING AHEAD

1. Trouble Is Coming to Tenisa

To the east of Bingola there was a country named Tenisa. The problems in Bingola started to spill over the border into Tenisa and people there began to discuss what would happen to their own country. There was real concern that civil war might soon break out.

Joseph Rana was a Catholic priest working in Tenisa. As he looked at the deteriorating political situation, he wondered if there was any way that he should be preparing his parish for future troubles, but he wasn't quite sure what to do. One day he was invited to the capital to take part in a conference on preventing AIDS. The organizers of the conference had invited a number of pastors from Bingola to come and share their experiences in preventing the spread of the disease. Everyone was interested and involved in the sessions during the day, but in the evenings when they sat and chatted, the main topic was what was going to happen in Tenisa.

One evening they listened to the news on the radio and were all very concerned that it seemed war could break out very soon. Pastor Peter from Bingola was sitting with them and he said: "When the war came to our country, we had an idea it was coming for a number of months. Later I wished so much that we had prepared our Christians for what was to come, but at the time we had no idea how to do this. I could give you some ideas about how to prepare for trouble if you like."

One of the other Tenisa pastors spoke up: "If we go home and start preparing our people for war, won't the government say that we are wanting the war to come? Or even that we are the ones behind the war?" "Not if you are careful in the way you do it," said Pastor Peter. The whole group agreed that this was a good thing, and for three evenings, Peter went over the preparations they could make, both from a practical point of view and also to prepare people spiritually.

At the end of the conference the participants all went home, and Father Joseph immediately started sharing what he had learned with the Christians. Many of them made practical preparations like packing up some medicines and other essential items ready to take at a moment's notice. They also discussed and made a plan how to warn the whole community when there was danger. In church, they started a series of Bible studies entitled "What if...?" They thought through what situations might arise and how they might handle them. Included in these studies were Scripture passages that addressed subjects like lying, murder and rape. They discussed what they would do if someone told them to kill another person or they would be killed, and other similar questions.

Two months later war broke out in Tenisa and Father Joseph's congregation scattered into the bush. Life was very hard for everyone. After a year, peace was restored to the country, and people were able to go back home and rebuild their lives. The first week that most people were back home, Father Joseph had a stream of people coming to greet him. Every single one wanted to tell him that the preparation they did together for trouble helped them so much. One man said, "If you hadn't told us to have a packet of medicines ready to take, most of my family would have died in the bush!" Another said, "Those studies about "What if..." helped me so much. When a rebel soldier told me to kill my wife, I knew I must refuse. In the end, God delivered us all."

❁ DISCUSSION QUESTION

Is it right to prepare for future trouble? Can you think of any Scriptures that say we should do this?

What troubles might you be unprepared for in your area?

2. Why Should We Prepare for the Future?

God's word says, "A prudent man sees danger and takes refuge, but the simple keep going and suffer for it" (Prov 22:3). God has given us intelligence and common sense and he expects us to use them. Church leaders are responsible before God to lead and look after their church congregations (Acts 20:26-31; Jer 23:1).

People in the middle of a crisis often don't have the ability to think in a clear way. If a decision has been made beforehand when there was time to study what God teaches, then it is much easier to do the right thing when the crisis comes. For example, one man from a war-torn country was threatened with death if he didn't kill his child. In the crisis of the moment he did as they said. Later, he was very distressed and said, "If only I had thought about this beforehand, I would never have killed my child."

Plans can also be developed for situations including natural disasters. For example, if a community lives near a volcano, or in an area subject to flooding, plans can be made as a community as to what could be done to help prepare for a flood or a volcano erruption.

Sometimes government officials may think that the church leaders are getting involved with politics when they discuss this type of preparation with their congregations. Depending on the local situation, it may be good to talk with local officials about this. Indeed, they should be involved in contingency plans for a village or a community, if possible. This may help them see the goodwill of the Church.

There are two areas of preparation that are important: practical and mental/spiritual.

3. How Can We Prepare Practically?

✿ DISCUSSION QUESTION

> *In groups of four, imagine the following situation: Your family is told that within thirty minutes they must leave to run into the bush. They can only take what they can carry. Make a list of the most important items to take and share this with the whole group.*

Some things that are important to take when fleeing are:
- Medicines
- Food, including salt
- Water
- Matches
- Cooking pot
- Identity papers
- Knife and/or machete
- Radio and batteries
- Bible
- Extra clothes

According to the local situation, other items will be added such as a cell phone. If a family really only had thirty minutes to get ready, they would very probably leave some important items behind. The best thing to do if a family thinks there is trouble coming, is to prepare a suitcase or a bag or a tied-up bundle with the essential items in it. Then this can be collected very quickly if the family needs to leave. All the above items except the radio (which is probably in daily use), could be put into the bag ready to go. There are various ways of preparing food so that it will not spoil. In some situations, it would be best to hide this bag in some other place where the family expects to go in case of trouble.

The church leaders also needs to think about church belongings. If possible, they need to take the most important documents with them. In some situations, it could be dangerous for a list of church members or other church documents to fall into the wrong hands.

For both the families and for the church, large heavy items that are important but cannot be taken should be hidden. Wrapping things up well and burying them in the ground seems to be one of the best ways to hide things. Be sure a number of people know where the item is buried!

4. How Can We Communicate When Trouble Comes?

A. With our families

Each family should openly discuss the danger they see coming. This discussion should include the children (See Lesson 4). The family should have some ideas and plans where they will go in case of danger. They should decide on a meeting place if the family gets separated and discuss different routes to get there. It is very important that even very small children are capable of saying their name and their family name. Even a three year old can learn to do this. In an East African war where many families were separated, children who could clearly give this information were reunited with their parents much more rapidly than children who only knew their first name. This has also been true in cases of natural disasters such as the tsunami in Asia.

B. With the churches and the community

In a certain West African country, the pastor of a church heard that enemies from another ethnic group were coming to the village. He rang the church bell and everyone came running to the church. This made them an easy target for the enemies, and many people were killed in the church. Generally speaking, rather than calling people to come to the church, it is better to have a way of ringing the church bell (or drum) which means, "Leave the village!" This should be discussed beforehand so that people are ready to leave in small groups to arranged destinations.

If there is more than one church in a village, it is very important that the church leaders get together and make a common plan. This should also involve community leaders. In a large town, plans should be made in each area of the town.

Does your community have a plan of what to do if enemy soldiers are approaching the village/town or if a natural disaster occurs? If you do not, who should be involved in discussing these plans?

C. With the outside world

When trouble comes to an area it is very important to have a way of making this known to the outside world. This may be done with media contacts, or by contacting those who have prayed for the people in that area, or through local NGOs, both Christian and non-Christian ones. This will help bring aid to the area and may help bring an end to the conflict.

5. How Can We Prepare Spiritually for Difficult Situations?

Divide into small groups and have each group discuss one of the questions below. Remember that non-literate people can also take part, but be sure to read the Scripture passage a number of times so that they can absorb the contents.

A. *What if a soldier tells you to kill someone or he will kill you?*

Read Revelation 21:1-7 and Exodus 20:13 and discuss the following questions.
1. What will happen to Christians when they die?
2. What does God say about murder?

Heaven is a much better place than earth. If a Christian is killed, that is not the worst thing that can happen! A person is made in the image of God. To kill someone is very wrong in God's sight.

B. *What if a soldier demands that you give him everything you have money and so on?*

Read Mathew 6:24-33, Hebrews 10:34, and Luke 12:15. Then discuss the following questions:

1. What does Jesus teach about possessions in the Mathew passage?
2. The writer to Hebrews says that they have accepted something gladly. What was that?
3. Jesus says that our lives are not tied up in what?

People whom God has made matter much more than material goods. Goods can be replaced later on; people cannot. We should be willing to give up our possessions rather than be killed.

C. *What if the enemies say you must denounce Christ in order to stay alive?*

   Read Mark 8:31-9:1, Acts 4:18-22, and Rev 3:7-10. Then discuss the following questions:
   1. In the Mark passage what does Jesus say his followers must do?
   2. What does Jesus say about someone who tries to hold on to his own life rather than following Jesus?
   3. In the Acts passage, why did Peter and John refuse to obey the religious leaders?
   4. In the Revelation passage, why did Jesus praise the church of Philadelphia?

It is never right to deny that we follow Christ, but sometimes this can be very difficult. If we do deny Christ, remember that if later we truly repent, God does forgive us. Think of the story of Peter.

D. *What if you are hiding people from an ethnic group who are being killed, and their enemies come to your house. If they ask where these people are, will you answer truthfully?*

Read Joshua 2:1-16. Then discuss the following questions:

1. Why did the spies come to Jericho? Who sent them?
2. Why did Rahab lie to the officials of Jericho?

3. Was she right to lie? Why or why not?

There may be special cases where it is right to deceive those who are against God. However this needs careful discussion so as not to give the idea that it is usually right to tell lies.

E. *Some other "what if..." situations that may be helpful for your community to discuss:*
   1. What if a soldier tells a man to rape a woman on pain of death?
   2. What if soldiers make a person eat human flesh on pain of death?
   3. What if you are captured by the rebels? How will you behave?
   4. If soldiers attack your family, can you defend yourselves?

There may be other situations to add according to your situation.

6. What Are Some General Points that May Help?

1. Promise together beforehand that no-one will kill another person.
2. Do not panic in the face of danger but quickly say a short prayer.
3. Memorise some Scripture passages beforehand that will help in these difficult situations.
4. Cooperate with other Christians; work together for everyone's safety. Particularly protect children and the elderly.

CLOSING SMALL GROUP EXERCISE

As we look into the future, no one can know what will happen. Even if we plan ahead, we can never be sure how we will behave in a crisis. But we do know God wants us to prepare and will be with us, even in pain and suffering. Share your hopes and fears for the future, and pray for each other and for your community.

FINAL CEREMONY

Participants will need a small piece of paper and a pen or pencil. The cross from Lesson 8 will be needed again, as well as a way to burn the papers. Seminars should close with a communion service, if possible.

1. Knowing God's Healing

The leader should remind the participants of the exercise "Taking Your Pain to the Cross." He should ask if there are other wounds that they have in their hearts that need healing. Some time should be given for silent prayer, and then the leader should pray for God's healing and blessing on everyone.

2. Repenting from Personal Sin and Knowing God's Forgiveness

The leader should read the following verses aloud:

1 John 1:8-10

If we say that we have no sin, we deceive ourselves, and there is no truth in us. But if we confess our sins to God, he will keep his promise and do what is right: he will forgive us our sins and purify us from all our wrongdoing. If we say that we have not sinned, we make a liar out of God, and his word is not in us.

Isaiah 53:5-6

But because of our sins he was wounded,
beaten because of the evil we did.
We are healed by the punishment he suffered,
made whole by the blows he received.
All of us were like sheep that were lost,

each of us going his own way.
But the LORD made the punishment fall on him,
on the punishment all of us deserved.

✿ Exercise

1. Ask forgiveness for any sins you know you have committed.
    Each person takes time alone to ask God to show him any sins that
    have not been forgiven yet. These may have happened during a
    war or conflict, or just as part of ordinary life. The sin may be against
    someone from another ethnic group or a family member or friend.
    Write these down on a piece of paper.

2. Know God's forgiveness for these sins.
    The leader says a prayer that acknowledges God's forgiveness for
    those who have repented. The following prayer from the Anglican
    prayer book could be used:

    > Almighty and most merciful Father,
    > we have erred and strayed from your ways like lost sheep,
    > we have followed too much the devices and desires of our own
    > hearts,
    > we have offended against your holy laws,
    > we have left undone those things which we ought to have done,
    > and we have done those things which we ought not to have done.
    > But you, O Lord, have mercy upon us,
    > spare those who confess their faults,
    > restore those who are penitent,
    > according to your promises declared to mankind
    > in Christ Jesus our Lord;
    > and grant, O most merciful Father, for his sake,
    > that we may hereafter live a godly, righteous, and sober life,
    > to the glory of thy holy Name. Amen.

3. Forgiving Others

The leader should give a brief summary of Lesson 9, remind-
ing them of what is forgiveness and what forgiveness is not, and
why God wants us to forgive people. Then he reads Romans
12:17-21 aloud:

If someone has done you wrong, do not repay him with a wrong. Try to do what everyone considers to be good. Do everything possible on your part to live in peace with everybody. Never take revenge, my friends, but instead let God's anger do it. For the scripture says, "I will take revenge, I will pay back, says the Lord." Instead, as the scripture says: "If your enemies are hungry, feed them; if they are thirsty, give them a drink; for by doing this you will make them burn with shame." Do not let evil defeat you; instead, conquer evil with good.

EXERCISE

1. *Each person should take time alone to think and pray about others they need to forgive. Write these down on a piece of paper.*
2. *Everyone returns to the group. Some people may wish to publicly forgive someone, or to confess sins against a particular ethnic group. This should not be forced, but the opportunity should be given.*

4. Bring Your Sin and Unforgiveness to the Cross

Bring the paper on which you wrote your sin and unforgiveness to the cross. Nail it to the cross, or put it in the box at the foot of the cross. As you do, say, "I'm handing over my sins to Jesus who died on the cross for me."

When all the papers have been deposited, take them outside and burn them. This shows that our sins are forgiven and that we have forgiven others.

5. Final Closing Moments

It is very good to finish with a communion service where everyone together praises God for his forgiveness and for their oneness in Christ.

Recommended Readings

Amalembe, Wilfred, et. al, eds, Growing Together: A Guide for Parents and Youth, Nairobi, Kenya: MAP International, 1996.

Campbell, D. Ross, How to Really Love Your Child, Elgin, IL: David C. Cook, 2004.

Cloud, Henry and John Townsend, How People Grow: What the Bible Reveals about Personal Growth, Grand Rapids, MI: Zondervan Books, 2001.

Dortzbach, Debbie, AIDS in Kenya: The Church's Challenge and the Lessons Learned, Nairobi, Kenya: MAP International, 1998.

Hughes, Selwyn, How to Help a Friend, Great Britain: CWR, 1994.

_____ Your Personal Encourager: Biblical Help for Dealing with Difficult Times, Great Britain: CWR, 1994.

Kilbourn, Phyllis, ed., Healing the Children of War: A Handbook for Ministry to Children Who Have Suffered Deep Traumas, Monrovia, California: MARC Publications, 1995.

Lloyd, Rhiannon and Kristine Bresser, Healing the Wounds of Ethnic Conflict: The Role of the Church in Healing, Forgiveness, and Reconciliation, Unpublished manuscript.

Sinclair, N. Duncan. Horrific Traumata: A Pastoral Response to the Post-Traumatic Stress Disorder. N.Y: Haworth Pastoral Press, 1993..

Tabifore, Henry and Sam Mulyanga, How to Teach Children Sexuality: A Handbook for Parents and Teachers, Alpha & Omega Publications, Nairobi, Kenya.

Willard, Dallas, The Divine Conspiracy: Rediscovering our Hidden Life in God, San Francisco: Harper Collins, 1998.

Yoder, Carolyn, The Little Book of Trauma Healing: When Violence Strikes and Community Security is Threatened, Intercourse, PA: Good Books, 2005.

Both MAP International and Paulines Publications Africa have significant resources for the Church in the area of how to respond to the challenges of HIV/AIDS.

MAP International
P.O. Box 21663
00505 Nairobi, Kenya.
E-mail: mapesa@map.org
Website: www.map.org

Paulines Publications Africa
Daughters of St Paul,
P.O. Box 49026, 00100 Nairobi, Kenya.
E-mail: publications@paulinesafrica.org
Website: www.paulinesafrica.org